The Coach's Coach

Personal development for personal developers

'It's all very well having coaches telling you how to do this and that, but ultimately it has to come from within.'

Ronnie O'Sullivan, 2004 Embassy World Snooker Champion, from his autobiography *Ronnie* (2004)

The Chartered Institute of Personnel and Development is the leading publisher of books and reports for personnel and training professionals, students, and all those concerned with the effective management and development of people at work. For details of all our titles, please contact the publishing department:

Tel: 020-8612 6204

E-mail: publish@cipd.co.uk

The catalogue of all CIPD titles can be viewed on all the CIPD website:

www.cipd.co.uk/bookstore

The Coach's Coach
Personal development for personal developers

Alison Hardingham

with

Mike Brearley, Adrian Moorhouse and Brendan Venter

Chartered Institute of Personnel and Development

Published by the Chartered Institute of Personnel and Development,
151 The Broadway, London SW19 1JQ

First published 2004
Reprinted 2005
Reprinted 2006 (twice)

Designed and typeset by Fakenham Photosetting, Fakenham, Norfolk
Printed in Great Britain by The Cromwell Press, Trowbridge, Wiltshire

British Library Cataloguing in Publication Data
A catalogue of this manual is available from the British Library

ISBN 1 84398 075 4

Chartered Institute of Personnel and Development,
151 The Broadway, London SW19 1JQ
Tel: 020 8612 6200
Email: cipd@cipd.co.uk   Website: www.cipd.co.uk
Incorporated by Royal Charter. Registered Charity No. 1079797

Contents

List of figures

List of photographs

Acknowledgements

First of all, I should like to acknowledge the contribution that Mike, Adrian and Brendan have made to this book. Their diversity and wisdom, which result from many years of trying to be the best they can possibly be and of helping others to do the same, have enhanced and broadened the scope of this book immeasurably. Their support and encouragement have made writing it fun, and given me the confidence that it is worth producing yet another book on coaching!

Then I should like to acknowledge all the people I have coached and those I am coaching still. One of the pleasures of writing this book has been the opportunity to call to mind everyone whom I have been privileged to coach, and reflect on the work we have done together. So I have spent the past few months surrounded by people bringing about positive changes in their working lives; I couldn't have asked for better company. You have coached me over many years in optimism and determination – very necessary qualities for a writer. Thank you.

I should also like to acknowledge Lois Whittaker and Stephen Partridge at the CIPD. The book was Lois's idea, and it shows her skill in bringing together very different people to make something new and interesting. Stephen is my editor, and his enthusiasm and pragmatism, combined with patience and a great sense of humour, have been absolutely essential to bringing the project to completion.

My commitment to coaching stems in no small part from the help and support I have been given at different times in my own personal and professional development by wise and loving counsellors. I should like to acknowledge specifically the influence of Kirsten Blow, Salvador Minuchin and Liz Standish, without whom my life today would be so much less than it is.

My son Ian has contributed to this book in two totally different ways. First, he is my 'technical support'; thanks, Ian, for being on hand when my computer and I weren't getting along. Second, as we all know, 'children are sent into the world to educate their parents'; thanks again, Ian, for taking the job seriously!

Last but not least, my thanks go to my partner, Claudio. His unconditional love and support underpin so much of what I do, and are the bedrock of this book.

Preface

Our aims

This is a book with two aims. The first is to help people who coach coach better. The second is to help people find better, and more, coaching for themselves.

Interest in coaching has grown phenomenally over the past decade or so. The idea of coaching used to be confined to the worlds of education and sport, but now we have introduced it into every aspect of life where people strive to do better and make the most of themselves; and that turns out to be, nowadays, every single aspect of life. Maybe this extension of coaching reflects our increasing preoccupation with achieving our full potential here on earth. Maybe it reflects the individualism that dominates current Western societies: individuals need individualised help to achieve their goals. Maybe it is just a new word for what has always been an important part of human experience – one person helping another through conversation to achieve their hopes, fulfil their wishes and live their dreams.

I don't want to get side-tracked in this Preface into a lengthy debate on how to define coaching. Coaching relationships evolve over time as each party understands the other better and understands what can be achieved through a particular coaching relationship, and what cannot be. In a similar way, I hope the understanding of coaching that I and my fellow contributors to this book have will become apparent through the pages of the book.

However, it's a good idea to have a little clarity at the start. A coach is someone who helps another person or group of people articulate and achieve their goals, through conversation with them. Coaching happens whenever that happens; and it happens all the time, not just in meetings with people who carry the title of 'coach'. When I ask groups of people to think about those in their lives who have coached them most effectively, they often mention their mother or their father. And equally often, they mention someone who said something once that helped them move forward, even though their path may never again have crossed that person's.

The contributors

Alison Hardingham, the main author, is a business psychologist and published author in the fields of management development and applied psychology. She has over 20 years of experience in coaching individuals and teams. Brendan Venter was an international rugby player who represented the South African national team, and subsequently played and coached at London Irish. He is now a GP in Cape Town. Adrian Moorhouse broke the world record in breast stroke five times and won an Olympic gold medal. He is now the managing director of Lane 4, a consulting company. Mike Brearley was one of England's best known and most successful cricket captains and is now a full-time psychoanalyst.

Already you will see that in this book we want to acknowledge and embrace the diversity of coaching. That is one of the reasons we are a diverse group of contributors. We come from the worlds of business, psychology, psychoanalysis, sport (both individual and team), and medicine; we include the male and the female perspective; we are young, middle-aged and old; we belong to profoundly different cultures; we have diverse pasts and diverse present lives; and the coaching experiences we have had are different.

Our challenge is to extract the core of understanding from that diversity and communicate it to you in a way that increases the choices open to you. I mean, choices about how to coach well, or how to find good coaching. We are against rule books and restriction; we are for excellence and integrity.

We chose to write this book together because we are interested in what coaching across many different fields of human endeavour has in common. We are also interested in the differences. The similarities and differences between coaching in sport and coaching in business are of particular importance. Business has borrowed a great deal from the expertise of sports coaches. There is indeed much to learn by comparing the two fields and yet many mistakes to be made if messages from sport are applied to business unthinkingly. So we have worked together to ensure that what we say here about the pillars of effective coaching is true for all the good coaching we have seen.

We have used our diversity of experience to illustrate our points with many different stories, from our different worlds. We hope you will enjoy the variety and breadth that these stories bring to the book.

And we believe in the coaching value of storytelling, as you will read later in this book.

The structure of the book

There are five parts to the book. All of us who have contributed have found our own lives immeasurably enhanced by the coaching we have done. People who have experienced good coaching (and that includes us too) say the same. In the first, second and third parts we aim to celebrate and capture that experience in a way that means more good coaching will happen more often.

So the book starts with the most important person in the coaching relationship, the coachee. What hopes and fears does he or she bring to coaching? How will their previous experiences and state of mind help or hinder the coaching effort?

The book then moves on to the coach. We explore what it is in the coach that makes good coaching possible, and what it is in him or her that makes good coaching impossible.

The third part looks at the nature of the coaching relationship. It includes thoughts about what flows from coachee to coach, as well as what flows from coach to coachee.

The fourth part is different in kind from the first three, and it is the longest part of the book. It describes the different kinds of work coach and coachee do together, and tools and techniques for approaching each kind of work successfully.

In the first four parts we have, for simplicity, taken most of our examples and illustrations from the context of one-to-one coaching in a business context. The fifth and final part of the book explores a number of other business contexts in which coaching takes place, and how those contexts affect what is possible and desirable in the coaching relationship. We hope these chapters will enable you to supply and obtain good coaching wherever you are.

The style of the book

We have written this book in a conversational style. We wanted to mirror coaching itself in the way the book was written, so that those who read it feel they are having an experience of being coached (a somewhat one-sided experience, it is true, but we have tried to imagine all the stories, questions and challenges you would be posing us as we wrote!). The book is narrative rather than didactic in style, although we hope our diversity and breadth of experience lend authority to the conclusions we draw. Our aim is that in reading this book you will feel you have been having a conversation with us, a conversation that increases your own passion for coaching and ability to do it – or receive it – well. Just as Ronnie O'Sullivan says in the quotation that opens this book, it would be 'all very well' our telling you to 'do this and that'; instead, we wanted to write a book that enabled you to access and act on your own thoughts and beliefs about coaching.

Just like a good coaching relationship, the book addresses philosophical issues of belief and value as well as practical issues of how to do things better. As a good coach links suggestions and reflections back to a coachee's own values and purpose, so we have tried always to link anything we recommend back to the fundamental purposes of coaching.

Coaching does not happen in a neat structured sequence. It is something that evolves and takes different turns. Everything is connected to everything else. So it has been hard to impose the linear structure of a book on this subject. We have tried to make links all the time between different parts of the book, so although there are distinct chapters, which can be read on their own, the underlying threads that run through the whole book are clear.

Finally, we have approached the problematic issue of gender by using 'he' and 'she' randomly throughout the book. Sometimes the coach is a 'he', sometimes a 'she', and for the sake of clarity the coachee is usually the opposite gender.

Protecting privacy

As we have said above, we believe in stories. We believe in their power to unite people in shared experience and to move us on through seeing how someone else has moved on. So there are many stories woven through our text. We have, as you would expect us to, protected the privacy of the people in the stories by changing details that are unimportant to the story, details such as gender, profession, organisation, and so on. Some of Mike's, Adrian's and Brendan's sporting stories involve well-known 'personalities', who are happy to be identified, but generally it is impossible to identify the 'real' person.

But the stories are nonetheless real.

PART ONE

THE COACHEE

Introduction

The whole point of coaching is to help the coachee. Throughout the coaching process, it is the coachee who needs to be at the centre of things. That is one of the characteristics of a coaching relationship that makes it so special. How often do we experience another person's intention and attention entirely focused on us and our goals? Most of social life is about trades, trade-offs, compromise and negotiation. We find a path that is acceptable to both parties if not ideal for either.

But coaching is one of those special asymmetric relationships (like therapy and the best kinds of teaching) where one individual puts his own preoccupations and needs aside in order better to understand and respond to the preoccupations and needs of another. So it is appropriate that this book should start with the coachee.

Chapter 1

Starting points

Introduction

In this chapter, we look at what has gone on for the coachee before she even has the first coaching session. What brings people to coaching? What are the 'best' starting points (that is, most likely to lead to a successful coaching outcome) and what are the 'worst' (most likely to undermine the coaching before it's even begun)? Coaches need to remember – and the good ones always do – that although for them coaching begins when the meeting takes place, for the coachee it will have already begun.

As James Flaherty (1999) puts it so succinctly and well: 'People are always and already in the middle of something.' So coaches must begin by understanding what it is that their coachees are already in the middle of, and by enabling them to understand how the coaching process will fit in the context of their up-and-running worlds.

Coaching: chosen or 'prescribed'?

The most important thing to understand when someone decides to receive coaching is whether she feels she is doing it freely, because she has chosen to, or whether she feels she has to some extent been 'forced' into it. Of course, as so often with issues to do with people, it is the coachee's perception of choice or coercion that matters more than any objective truth about whether she has chosen freely. In fact, most people will come to the coaching process conscious of a mix of choice and coercion.

Mike Brearley puts it well, drawing on his varied experiences of coaching and being coached: 'It is a mistake to think that everyone, all the time, wants to change, or wants to learn; or again, is open to learning from me.' On the one hand, we all want to develop, to become more than we are, and we move towards coaching freely. On the other hand, we should all prefer it if we were naturally competent and successful in every way, without needing any coaching.

So to some extent every coachee is 'forced into coaching' by external events or people, which demonstrate the difference between what she wants to be and what she is. For example, I should like to be able to just sit and write this book with no help. But I suspect that the progress of the book and feedback from my editor will lead me to seek coaching from friends, colleagues, and my fellow contributors. So I shall come to that coaching feeling mostly that I have freely chosen it, but also feeling a tinge of doing it 'against my will'.

Why do coaches need to be concerned with this issue of choice? The point is, coaching is about helping another person achieve their goals. The single most important achievement of any coach is to leave the coachee feeling more confident in, and more committed to, herself (more of this and of how to do it later). Effective coaching produces an increase of will, of self-determination, and of self-belief, in the coachee. So if the coachee feels that entering coaching is itself an act against her will, it will be much harder for the coach to achieve that central outcome. Yet it is important to recognise that some ambivalence about coaching will be there most of the time for all our coachees, and not just at the start of coaching.

So what do we do? We ask permission to coach. That puts the coachee back in charge, and leads her to perceive, rightly, that it is she who will determine what happens as a consequence of coaching. In fact, in every coaching conversation coaches must be concerned with what they have 'permission' to do. The more coercion the coachee has felt

The more coercion the coachee has felt in coming to coaching, the more carefully a coach will need to ensure that that permission is there and that it continues.

in coming to coaching, the more carefully a coach will need to ensure that that permission is there and that it continues. But even with coachees who have made pretty much a free choice, the issue of permission is still relevant.

Towards one end of the choice spectrum from the example of me and my writing would be someone (and I have known many) who has had coaching 'recommended' to them as something that will enhance their promotion prospects. Right at the other end of the spectrum are those (and I have known one or two) who have been told to have coaching as part of a disciplinary procedure. That is pretty much total coercion.

Where there is a significant amount of coercion (either real or perceived by the coachee) then coaching itself cannot begin, and even if begun, cannot continue, without explicit permission-seeking by the coach. While it is fine to meet with someone to discuss coaching even if they have been 'told' to meet you, it is a waste of time, and disrespectful, to coach without the coachee wanting it.

So before anything else, the coach will need to find out from the coachee why he is there and explore whether there is something the coachee wants him to help with. This may take some time, and the most useful question for the coach in this process is 'Is there some way I can help you here?' Initially, the answer may be a more or less truculent 'I don't know – I don't have an idea of what you do'.

Then the coach will need to describe the sorts of things he might do, and that will lead to further discussion. Until the coach hears the coachee say, with conviction rather than compliance, 'Well, I should find it helpful if you/we . . .' the coaching hasn't yet reached a good starting point.

I have known this process of permission-seeking to take hours and span more than one session. Of course, there is value in the permission-seeking process itself, because it is helping the coachee become clear about what she feels and wants, which is in itself an important part of coaching. Sometimes the coach will do the coachee a great service when he realises that he wants neither coaching nor the consequence being held out as a 'reward' for coaching.

For example, I remember a lawyer to whom it was suggested she should seek coaching to prepare herself for the possibility of a managing partner role. I spent a couple of hours with her, at the end of which she concluded that she wanted that role 'on her own terms' or not at all; she did not want any coaching.

Even in cases of 'total coercion', coaching may still be very effective, if the permission-seeking is done properly. In fact, sometimes coaching that has such apparently inauspicious beginnings turns out to be the most productive of all, because coach and coachee are forced from the outset to acknowledge the coachee's reluctance to change and to plan together what to do about that reluctance.

I remember a banker who had 'failed' a promotion board and in consequence been given a series of coaching sessions with me. Had we begun without proper permission-seeking, we would have focused immediately on the areas the board had identified as 'weak': people management and relationship-building with his peers. But during the course of our permission-seeking conversation, he expressed his view:

that the board had been badly run and that in any case his excellent track record showed he was in fact fully competent on every dimension the board was supposed to assess. He didn't see what coaching could do for him.

We spent a session or two talking about all this, and he ended up deciding that he wanted to try for promotion again the following year. He asked that our coaching focus on how he could make as sure as possible that he would 'pass' next time. Not only did he indeed pass the following year, but as the coaching unfolded he became increasingly interested in improving his general management skills and sorting out some work relationships that had been problematic for some time.

If this banker had been plunged straight into a coaching agenda he didn't agree with, he would have been trapped. If he had stuck to his self-belief (that he didn't need coaching), he wouldn't have been able to take advantage of the coaching and develop. If he had responded to coaching, his confidence in his own understanding of himself would have been damaged. The permission-seeking process enabled him to find his own way to make sense of and use the coaching opportunity; it allowed him to develop and to keep his self-respect.

Mike Brearley adds to this central point about permission-seeking. He has found that timing is often critical. He tells a story from his own experience when too much coaching was given at the wrong time.

> 'I was a poor golfer. I once went round with Ted Dexter and two others. I did really well for half a round, until Ted started coaching me. I have no doubt that what he said was right. But the timing wasn't, and I was rapidly hooking and slicing to an alarming degree. ...

> 'I remembered this experience when, as captain of England on tour in Pakistan, I questioned Ken Barrington's attempt to coach the Somerset opening batsman, Brian Rose, into a different kind of grip and backlift.

> 'I was very aware of how few Brian's chances were likely to be, and how radical the coaching advice sounded. He had after all got to where he was with his closed backlift, and trying to change it in the limelight and the short term of a tour was, I thought, asking for trouble.'

So there will be times when a coachee is ready for coaching, and times when she is not. Also, there will be times when she is ready for 'radical' coaching, and times when that is the last thing she needs or wants. We need to be sensitive to all of this when we are seeking permission to coach, and, as Mike Brearley puts it, we need as coaches to 'stay with the person, be willing to get stuck in over time'.

One final point on this issue of whether the coachee has truly chosen to be coached. You won't know until you talk with the coachee herself. I can't count the number of times I have been told by someone's boss that so-and-so is 'delighted' at the prospect of coaching, only to discover that so-and-so is confused about what coaching means and a bit put out at the implication she needs to improve!

An informed choice?

Coachees vary greatly in terms of how much they know about coaching. And there are two relevant aspects to knowledge here. One is general knowledge about what coaching is, what its goals and possibilities are, and what the process entails.

The other is knowledge about a specific coach, what his style is likely to be and how he may be particularly helpful. Where a coachee has already experienced coaching, she may have a good general idea of what she is embarking on, although with no, or even the wrong, idea about how her new coach will go about things.

Similarly, where a coachee has chosen to be coached by someone she knows in another context (perhaps she has seen him on a training course, or he is an old boss or current colleague), she may have a pretty good idea of how that person will behave but much less of an idea of what having a coaching relationship with that person might offer. For all coachees at the start of a new piece of coaching there will be some uncertainty and so some apprehension.

It is the coach's job to give the coachee as much information as she needs to relax and take her place as an equal partner in the coaching relationship. I remember a very senior partner in a firm of chartered surveyors whose HR director (with whom he was very friendly) had suggested he have coaching with me because he was about to drown under the pressures of his workload. He trusted his colleague and friend enough to agree to a meeting with me, but he had no real idea of what she was suggesting and he was clearly extremely ill at ease when he came into the room to meet me.

It was a room at his work, and had in it a large round table with six chairs. I was already seated, and he sat as far away from me as possible, with a whole expanse of table between us. I spent most of the first session just talking with him about coaching and my approach, and thankfully when he came to the second session he chose a chair much closer to me!

Of course, there is also the question 'how well-informed is the coachee as to how coaching could help in relation to her specific issue?' This is something that also has to be explored early on. Because having an executive coach has become something of a fashion and also in some organisations a 'badge of seniority', a coachee may occasionally opt for coaching without herself having a clear objective for the process.

I was referred a banker recently who said he wanted coaching because it would be interesting and he'd never tried it. Also, I have sometimes had people referred to me when it is clear they need counselling or therapy; then the job is to help them find their way to that without becoming frightened about what such a course of action 'says about them'.

Triggers, discontinuities and 'breakdowns'

I start from the premiss that although a lot of coaching goes on, and that many of us experience a great deal and a great variety of coaching in our lives, nonetheless coaching is not continuous. It is episodic.

Each 'episode' of coaching has a beginning and an end. We need to be aware of what our coachees see as the 'beginning' of an episode where we are their coach, and we also need to be alert to possible beginnings for ourselves and for others. That way we shall use coaching opportunistically, and 'just in time', and it is then that coaching is most likely to be effective.

> Each 'episode' of coaching has a beginning and an end. We need to be aware of what our coachees see as the 'beginning' of an episode where we are their coach, and we also need to be alert to possible beginnings for ourselves and for others.

The trigger for coaching is usually a perceived gap between what the coachee can do and what the coachee wants to do. Such a gap is felt by the coachee as a 'discontinuity', a 'breakdown' in the smooth running of her life. Coaching is, for the coachee, about bridging that gap, so that 'normal service can be resumed as soon as possible'!

The gap may be perceived because feedback has brought it to the coachee's attention. It may be perceived because the coachee is being asked to do something new that she has never been developed for. It may be perceived because the coachee has decided to set herself a new and ambitious goal.

Mike Brearley tells a good and very relevant story about a 'breakdown', which triggered an opportunity for him to coach Ian Botham when Mike was captaining England in the famous Headingley test of 1981. (It is generally considered that Mike played a major role in 'helping to rediscover Botham's mercurial talents' – so says Simon Hughes, *Guardian* sports correspondent – and his identification of, and response to, triggers for coaching was essential in this.)

Mike explains: 'The pitch was a shocker, and we were in a poor position. Botham went in to bat, summed it up, and decided, rightly, to

Mike Brearley (left) discusses tactics with Ian Botham during the 1981 Ashes series

go for his shots. After a few minutes he played a big forcing shot off the back foot against Lillee, and missed. He looked up at the players' balcony. I gestured to him that he should have tried to hit it harder. I was inviting him to keep going with the tide; I was letting the horse have its head.'

The 'breakdown' occurred when Botham found his batting didn't produce the effect he was looking for. At that moment, he was ready for some input, and he looked up at Mike. Interestingly, Mike responded with a light touch (probably all he could do from the balcony, but addressing the central issue of Botham's self-belief).

That brief and superficially insignificant event is considered by Mike, and others, to have been key in enabling Botham to perform as he wanted to. (And perform he did, scoring a sensational 149 not out and helping England produce one of the most remarkable victories, and certainly one of the most remarkable comebacks, in the history of test cricket.)

In many instances, the 'breakdown' occurs when the coachee perceives a gap between his own capability and the capability of someone he admires. For example, a senior manager told me he wanted to be like a friend of his, who was intelligent and astute about people, but accepting and non-judgmental. This manager recognised in himself a destructive tendency to 'write people off' if he judged them stupid or lazy.

A great deal of coaching happens when there is a major change in the coachee's work life. Many organisations use coaching at key transitions, from doer to manager, and from manager to leader, for example. Such transitions in role are likely to throw up significant 'gaps' of the kind we have been talking about. Also, a coachee will want to bridge the gap between wanting to do a good job generally in the new role, and knowing how to deploy her capabilities specifically to achieve that.

So long as the coachee's life is running along smoothly and predictably, she is unlikely to seek coaching. When the smooth running of our lives 'breaks down' (we can't get what we want, we have to change, we are overtaken by dissatisfaction and a desire for something new), then we become more open to coaching. As coaches, we welcome such opportunities to contribute to someone else's development and achievement; but the coachee is likely to be much more ambivalent about the need for coaching.

A part of her will be intrigued and even excited at the possibility of personal growth; another part of her will wish the need for it had never arisen. Recognising this ambivalence, so different from the coach's wholehearted and easy enthusiasm for the process so dear and so familiar to her, is essential if the coach is to make the best use of the coachee's starting point.

Chapter 2

Hopes and fears

Introduction

The hopes and fears people bring to a coaching relationship have a strong influence on what happens in the relationship, and need to be understood. In this chapter we look at the most common hopes and fears, how to recognise them, what their consequences are, and what the coach needs to do about them.

Appropriate hopes and fears

Whenever we enter a new relationship, there are things it is sensible to hope, and things it is sensible to fear. These hopes and fears help us to make the most of what the relationship has to offer, while protecting ourselves from harm.

So it is with coaching. Appropriate hopes for the coachee include hope of achieving a specific goal (to get promoted, to win the contest, and so on), hope of discovering something new and important about herself, hope of at last being able to do something she has struggled with for some time (make a presentation to large groups, keep her temper at all times at work) and hope of rediscovering her confidence in, and enjoyment of, work. Other appropriate hopes centre on the kind of relationship she is hoping for with the coach. She may hope that someone will listen to her without interrupting, that someone will show intelligent and sustained interest in her, that she will be challenged to think in new ways.

Some of the appropriate hopes I have come across and most enjoyed include an accountant hoping to rekindle his affection for the organisation he was a partner in, a lawyer hoping to rediscover his 'joie de vivre', and a publisher hoping to stop working a 90-hour week. Such hopes are the driving power of the coaching relationship. The more clearly defined they are, the more likely it is the coachee will achieve them. She simply won't give up, and won't let the coach give up, until she has. These appropriate hopes are things to be returned to by the coach again and again. They are not only the driving power; they are the guiding stars and the measures of success.

When there are no appropriate hopes, then maybe the coaching will never take off. I worry about coachees who 'don't hope for much'. I spend time kindling hope, exploring 'the best you could hope for', 'the thing which might happen if it works better than you could imagine', 'a crazy idea you have about what could happen that would be good'. Hope is the wellspring of coaching.

Appropriate fears include fear that the coach will not be skilful or attentive enough; that the coachee has misunderstood her own need and so will misdirect the coach; that the goal is too difficult; that coaching is the wrong way to make progress. Then there is the appropriate fear that the coach will put himself first not the coachee, that he might encourage her to become dependent on him, that time and money will be wasted.

The coachee may also, appropriately, fear that she is herself not serious enough about change, not diligent enough to do the 'homework' the coach sets, not open enough to give the coach the information he needs to do his job. All these fears spur coach and coachee on to check that as good a job as possible is being done.

I worry about coachees who enter coaching with absolute confidence it will be good. I worry they will not keep me, and themselves, up to the mark.

So hopes and fears are rightly at the heart of coaching. But where they become out of proportion, or unrelated to reality, they become inappropriate and undermine what coaching can achieve. Let's look at the most common of these, and at how to recognise and deal with them.

Hope of salvation

Some coachees are looking to be 'saved from themselves'. Often at an unconscious level, they hope to hand responsibility over to the coach for sorting out the parts of themselves that are holding them back. Warning signs that this kind of inappropriate hope is present are comments from the coachee such as 'Just tell me what to do', 'I'm sure you know better than me what's going on', and 'You must have dealt with a lot of cases like me'!

If as a coach you feel flattered, beware; you could be trapped into taking on more responsibility than is helpful. What coach and coachee need to keep at the forefront of their minds all the time is that coaching is about enabling the coachee, and for someone to be enabled they must be in charge.

The coachee will have her reasons for hoping someone else will deal with the things that block her. Maybe people around her have behaved in ways that sap her confidence. Maybe she has made progress in the past by finding someone she can idealise who then takes care of her progression. Maybe she is angry about having coaching at all (remember what we said about the ambivalence of coaches towards the coaching process), and so she is withdrawing her commitment to it by handing responsibility to the coach. The coach needs to respect her reasons, but get her into the driving seat. That becomes the first thing to be done, before any further progress can be made.

Questions are, as so often, the key. Questions emphasise what the coachee knows and the coach does not. They help both parties remember that the coachee always knows so much more than the coach. She knows history, context, the depth of her feelings, what she has tried and succeeded at, what she has tried and failed at. Questions about all this will restore the right equilibrium: coachee in charge, coach supporting.

Being like many people somewhat susceptible to flattery myself, I have nearly been caught on more than one occasion in the trap of believing I can save someone else. The most direct appeal to my fantasy of omnipotence came when a lawyer whom I had been coaching for some time said to me: 'I want what you've got. I want to be able to coach others in the way you do.'

Just in time I stopped myself launching into a little speech on how I do the wonderful things I do, complete with a set of handy tips. Had I done that, I would have placed myself firmly in charge of his coaching. Instead I embarked on exploring how he needed to coach, who he needed to coach, what exactly he needed to do differently, and where he had already been successful. A narrow escape – for him and me!

Sometimes the trap is more subtly set. If the coach finds herself talking a lot, or leaving a session feeling rather good about her own competence, or noticing that few ideas are coming from the coachee, then it's a good idea to check what's going on. It's easy to stray into saving someone from the nearby territory of helping them; the good news is, it's usually easy to move back again.

Acknowledging your mistake to the coachee is a good way to move back because it demonstrates in the most straightforward way that the coach is not infallible and is in fact dependent on a working partnership with the coachee to do good work. Such acknowledgement is readily achieved with comments such as 'I seem to be talking too much' or 'I think I've got myself into telling you what to do rather than exploring with you what you think you should do.'

Hope of being given 'the answer'

This hope is related to the hope of salvation but it is less to do with idealising the coach and more to do with wanting an easy life! Because most coachees have established behaviour patterns that have brought them success as well as held them back, because all these behaviours are part of an integrated whole and unlikely to be amenable to 'tweaking' and because coachees are part of complex social and organisational systems, change is unlikely to be simple. Coach and coachee need to work together, usually over some time, to chart a path that introduces new behaviours which fit.

Sometimes the coachee does have a sudden insight which results in pretty immediate change. Occasionally such an insight enables the coachee to reach her goal with no further ado. I remember a coachee of mine whose goal was to build a better relationship with her boss. Her sudden insight was that he wasn't her son! (He was younger than her and similar to her son in some ways, but of course she wasn't responsible for bringing him up!)

This insight certainly resulted in some instant change as she stopped nagging him and being irritated by what she saw as inappropriate behaviour. But the insight alone was not enough, because there were all sorts of reasons why she had chosen to treat him in a parental way, and these had to be understood too for any change to last.

Because most coachees have established behaviour patterns that have brought them success as well as held them back, because all these behaviours are part of an integrated whole and unlikely to be amenable to 'tweaking' and because coachees are part of complex social and organisational systems, change is unlikely to be simple.

Coach and coachee are both tempted by the hope for 'the answer'. But if it comes from the coach it can lessen the coachee's confidence in her own problem-solving ability. And people are not linear; we are webs of behaviour and intention. The hope of an 'answer' to something that is not a question or a puzzle but rather a pattern, a multi-faceted whole, seems likely to lead both coach and coachee down a blind alley.

Often things first get more complex as a result of coaching and only out of that increase in complexity does a way forward begin to emerge. If we make simplicity our goal we are likely to end up with facileness instead.

Fear of exposure

This is present in almost every coaching relationship and in almost every coaching session. It is strange in one sense to talk of it as an 'inappropriate' fear. It is appropriate for us to protect ourselves, to be alert to dangers to our position in the world and our self-esteem. But I am calling it inappropriate in this context nonetheless, because it gets in the way of effective coaching.

Let's consider first the fear of exposure to people outside the coaching sessions. It is to allay this fear that we give the guarantee of absolute confidentiality to our coachees. Without that guarantee, they will be unable to explore everything they need to during coaching. They will have to be 'watching their back'. They must be completely confident that what they say in the coaching sessions will never be revealed in an attributable way by the coach to anyone else.

Some people believe this fairly readily. Others never fully believe it, and it does restrict the benefit they get from coaching. All the coach can do is state it as a ground rule, explain why it matters to her as much as it matters to the coachee, and then stick to it.

There is another aspect to this fear. That is the fear of exposure to the coach, and the related fear of being exposed to yourself by the coach. There are questions we don't want to hear, because we know the answers and we're not ready to face them. There are words we don't want to hear ourselves saying, because for the time being we are hiding from the truth of them. So this fear is about self-protection.

Again, different people fear this to differing degrees. Those who can set this fear aside fairly readily can go further faster in the coaching relationship. Others always struggle with it, and so must go along more cautiously, with more constraints. A coach working with someone who has a strong fear of exposure to censure (the coach's or his own) will observe that the coachee chooses his words carefully, makes little forays into talking about something he feels embarrassed or ashamed about, backs off to safer ground, and sometimes exits coaching if he has pushed himself too far too soon.

This fear is in us all to some degree. It is inappropriate to the coaching relationship because it is the whole premiss of coaching that it will help the coachee to become stronger, more capable, and more confident. So if the fear is strongly present, it suggests that the coach is not doing a good job. Either that, or that the coachee is so self-protective that coaching is not a good process for her. Some people need to develop privately.

I would say most people can benefit from coaching, but not everyone. I remember an accountant who had one session and concluded it was not 'her way' to talk about these things. From what I hear, she has done well without coaching, and learned how to manage and lead people in some other more private way.

The important thing is for coach and coachee to be aware of this fear of exposure, of the limits it sets, and of when those limits have been exceeded. For the coachee to feel this fear in a sustained and/or intense way means something in the coaching has to change.

Fear of being controlled

The fear of being controlled is another of those fears that is healthy, and necessary for entering relationships with others without losing our sense of ourselves. But when it is too strong, it gets in the way of effective coaching.

Of course, it is incumbent on the coach to resist the temptation to take control. We have already talked about this in the paragraphs about the inappropriate hopes for salvation and an 'answer'. But for a coachee to get the most out of coaching, the coach has to be allowed to take a lead from time to time. This may be simply in deciding what should be talked about next, or it may be in setting 'homework' (tasks for the coachee to complete outside the sessions, to experiment with new approaches or to consolidate learning).

The coach may take the lead by stating clearly how things seem to her, or by disagreeing with a course of action the coachee proposes. (We talk more about this issue of sharing control in Chapter 9 on the key dynamics of the coaching relationship.)

A coachee who feels comfortable in control of himself and his life will be able to follow the coach's lead, try something out or reflect on some new idea, listen to and reflect on the coach's perspective on his issues. He will not agree with the coach just because she is the coach; but neither will he resist and reject the coach's input out of a worry that the coach is trying to take charge.

This kind of relaxed approach means the coach is free to speak her mind (while of course being respectful – but more of this in Part Two). And of course, the coachee is free to decide the coach is wrong. That is a part of good coaching.

But where the coachee argues all the time with the coach's views, without pausing to explore them first, then it is possible that his fear of being controlled has become too strong. Sometimes this happens when the coachee sees the coach as an agent of the organisation, as having a kind of managerial authority because 'management' has arranged the coaching for him. Then it is important to return to per-mission-seeking in the way we described above.

A type of fear of being controlled occurs when the coachee wonders if the coach is trying to encourage her to be dependent on him, the coach. Giving the coachee control over number and frequency of sessions, agreeing at the start how and when the coaching will end, agree-ing review points where the coachee reviews the coaching – all these things help to set such a fear aside.

My view, however, is that the best way to reduce and manage inap-propriate fears is through the coach being very aware of her own feel-ings and motivations at all times, and working hard to 'keep these clean'.

Most of us have well-developed antennae for whether others intend us ill or well. It is part of our biological inheritance as social animals who survive or die largely as a consequence of our relationships with others. So if the coach's intentions are completely positive towards the coachee, the coachee will sense this, and inappropriate fear will subside.

For this reason, there is much of relevance to this chapter on 'hopes and fears' in Part Two of this book, where we focus on the qualities of a good coach.

Chapter 3

'Life positions'

Introduction

The coachee is an active partner in the coaching process. His customary approach to life, his bedrock of beliefs and values about himself and others, and about himself in relation to others, will be very important in determining how he fulfils his part of the partnership. Some life positions are very conducive to good coaching; working with a coachee who has such a life position is usually straightforward and often a joy. Other life positions present problems for the coaching process, and the coach will need to recognise these and work hard to ensure they don't prevent the coachee gaining as much as possible from the coaching.

Different ways of understanding 'life position'

There are many ways to draw distinctions between different individuals' 'life positions', that is, the central core of beliefs and attitudes that govern those individuals' choices throughout life. (And by choices I mean choices about what to pay attention to and how to interpret what they see and hear as well as more obvious choices about what actions to take.)

There is, for example, the view that every one of us has a neurosis of some sort or another (a neurosis being an irrational and to some extent debilitating anxiety or set of anxieties) and that our life positions can be categorised according to which neurosis we have. Examples of the categories are: depressive (people who believe they can't make any real positive difference to their own lives); paranoid (people who believe other people mean them harm); and narcissistic (people who believe they need lots of attention to be paid to them all the time by just about everyone they meet).

While most of us have one or more of these neuroses to only a mild degree, and can live, relate to others and develop quite satisfactorily, nonetheless our governing neurosis has significant impact on the choices we make, and it will certainly affect how we enter and respond to a coaching process.

If we are slightly inclined towards the depressive neurosis, for example, we may be slow to take charge of our own goals, not having as much confidence as most that we can achieve them. If we are slightly inclined towards paranoia, our coach may need to work extra hard to overcome our fears of exposure and of being controlled.

Then there are the different life positions that result from different kinds of relationships with parents.

There is, for example, the life position originating from being the 'baby of the family', indulged and loved unconditionally. There is the life position that derives from being a first-born, the focus for all the parents' unfulfilled hopes and dreams. (These correspondences are not set in stone – not all last-born are indulged, for example – but they are common, and give a flavour of how relationship to parents can have effects on choices we make throughout our lives.) You might imagine that coaching someone who has been a classic 'baby of the family' would present different challenges from coaching a 'first-born'.

And let us not forget the different life positions of men and women, of people from the Western hemisphere and people from the East, of the young and the old, and so on.

A further – and my final – example of 'life positions' can be found in the psychoanalyst Jung's classification of 'psychological types', made widely accessible through the psychometric questionnaire the 'Myers–Briggs Type Indicator®' (MBTI). Although Jung was focusing on different ways of thinking about the world, rather than different ways of feeling about the world, his categories describe 16 personality types, which differ fundamentally in terms of what they consider to be the most important aspects of reality.

Some of us consider the future to be more important than the present, and pay much more attention to it, for example. Others of us consider logic and analysis to be more important than feelings and the preservation of values. Again, such differences will have profound implications for how a coachee will come to coaching and how coaching will work best for him.

It is vital for coach and coachee to be constantly exploring all the different 'life positions' the coachee takes, both those she is well aware of and those she holds initially at an unconscious level. It will be in these distinctive beliefs and attitudes about life that coach and coachee are most likely to discover both blocks to progress and spurs to progress.

To give a simple example, I remember a coachee who wanted to be more organised but despite plans, time management techniques and well-intentioned nagging by his secretary just could not bring about any change. We used the MBTI and discovered he paid attention almost exclusively to the future. Further exploration revealed that he believed a concern for order was evidence of a lack of imagination (a grievous flaw in the eyes of someone who pays attention exclusively to the future!).

So as part of the coaching process I suggested he embark on a study of all the people he admired. He discovered to his surprise that quite a few of them were not only creative but also very orderly and methodical. From that point on he became able to introduce a degree of order into his working life. He was working in a way that acknowledged and capitalised on an aspect of his own 'life position'.

In the rest of this chapter, I would like to focus on the psychiatrist Berne's four life positions, which are at the heart of his widely acknowledged and understood theory of human relationships, 'transactional analysis'. I have found these life positions to be strongly predictive of how easily and quickly effective coaching can be established. Also, an understanding of a coachee's life position helps the coach anticipate and overcome some of the most likely blocks.

Finally, Berne's formulation encompasses many of the finer distinctions that other categorisations draw. It allows us to hold a simple framework in our minds, and sensitises us to the huge differences in outlook between one coachee and another, without overwhelming us with complexity.

'I'm OK, You're OK'

When a coachee is operating from this life position, the coaching prognosis is very good. She believes she is an equal adult, shares responsibility readily, and has a basic confidence in herself that positions her well for developing. She is unlikely to be prey to unrealistic hopes or debilitating fears. She will be able to give and receive feedback, and learn from success and from failure.

Coaching can begin straightaway, and she is likely to feel she has made a positive choice in embarking on the process. On the whole, she will expect fairness and care from others around her, including her coach, and is likely to behave in ways that elicit such treatment from others.

When people operate according to 'I'm OK, you're OK', it usually means that their experience of life has on balance been good. It does not mean they have lived a life without pain or problems, but the significant relationships in their life have nourished them well, and there has been give and take appropriate to their age and role in relation to others.

Unless the coach damages the relationship through clumsiness or bad intent, it is unlikely there will be blocks to the success of coaching in her coachee's relationship with her.

How do you recognise that a coachee operates from 'I'm OK, you're OK'? She is open to ideas and suggestions, but not passively or uncritically; she enjoys exploring possible actions and their consequences with her coach. She gives her own views and asks for the coach's; she is open about what she is feeling; she observes the boundaries of the coaching relationship spontaneously.

But more than anything else, the coaching process feels 'clear'; the coach has no sense of hidden agendas, of unspoken concerns, or of manoeuvring and manipulation. The coach feels relaxed and the sessions are usually 'cool' – not 'cool' as in aloof, but 'cool' in the sense of rational and objective rather than emotional and subjective.

Smiles and laughter come easily to both coach and coachee, and communication seems straightforward. Misunderstandings are few, and spotted pretty much as soon as they occur. Acknowledgement of mistakes and failures by either party is easy.

Swimmer Adrian Moorhouse describes himself as a 'good coachee'. And the evidence would back that assertion up. He worked with the same coach from the age of 14 to 28, including times when they 'fell out' but then moved the coaching relationship to a different place and continued. (After all, he was growing up during that time.) He has also

> *When people operate according to 'I'm OK, you're OK', it usually means that their experience of life has on balance been good. It does not mean they have lived a life without pain or problems, but the significant relationships in their life have nourished them well.*

had many different coaches in addition to his main one, and tends to take something from every one, even though they have a whole range of styles and perspectives.

Adrian describes himself as 'comfortable being coached', happy for feedback and input, self-aware and inclined to look for anything that will help. These are hallmarks of the 'I'm OK, you're OK' coachee.

In short, the coach can get down to business, and so can the coachee.

'I'm OK, you're not OK'

There are three other life positions in Berne's formulation and they are all to some degree defensive. In other words, people in these life positions have had experiences that result in them feeling fundamentally threatened by others. To protect themselves, they have settled upon a particular way of relating to others.

A person who operates from 'I'm OK, you're not OK' has decided that attack is the best form of defence. She doesn't feel equal to others, so she behaves as if she were superior. With any luck, others will be so busy defending themselves against this, they won't have the opportunity to spot her inferiority (or so her unconscious reasoning goes). She puts herself forward and others down. She can be aggressive. She conceals her own weaknesses and failures, and exposes those of others. She behaves in a way that can make others feel inferior. She may blame others frequently.

With this life position, as with all the defensive life positions, the coach needs to work hard to establish and maintain equality with the coachee. The risk will be that the coach himself will be drawn into defensive behaviour, and try to establish his superiority when challenged or blamed by the coachee. But he has the opportunity to demonstrate equality, by acknowledging his own errors or limitations and exploring what impact they have had, and by using questions to arrive at a fuller understanding of what is going on, taking both parties' perspectives into account.

Here is an example of how this plays out. A coachee didn't like a piece of feedback her coach gave her. She criticised the coach for drawing a conclusion from her behaviour in the coaching session when 'after all, these sessions are nothing like meetings at work'. In other words, the coach was ignorant.

The coach may start talking about how behaviours like the coachee's tend to be the same across a variety of situations; he may produce examples and even research to support this. If he does that, he may have entered the 'I'm not ignorant; you are' game. Understandable, but counterproductive.

It would be better if he became curious about the coachee's criticism. What are the differences between her behaviour in coaching and outside? Why are those differences there? Are there similarities? And so on. The coach is skilfully steering the relationship back towards equality.

Openness is difficult for 'I'm OK, you're not OK' people. They need to maintain an illusion of superiority (remember, they really fear they are inferior) by concealing things about themselves. The coach needs to be prepared for this. His best approach is to demonstrate that he himself can be open and not become inferior. Where he has opportunity to disclose truths about himself that he might feel vulnerable about, he can begin to demonstrate just that.

(I am not suggesting the coach disclose a lot of personal information; that could easily be self-indulgent and get in the way of what the coachee needs to talk about. But he can acknowledge where he is at a loss as to what to suggest next, or where he feels he has said something unhelpful, or where he feels he hasn't yet understood something.)

The coach may in this way lead the coachee towards greater openness. He shows it is safe for him, and the coachee begins to feel it might be safe for her.

> *Openness is difficult for 'I'm OK, you're not OK' people. They need to maintain an illusion of superiority (remember, they really fear they are inferior) by concealing things about themselves. The coach needs to be prepared for this.*

'I'm not OK, you're OK'

This is the opposite of the previous defensive life position. It is based on the idea that the best form of defence is to give in. Other people are superior, so you subordinate your own wishes to theirs.

The signs are an inappropriate readiness to treat the coach as an expert, lack of challenge of the coach, immediate compliance with the coach's suggestions and requests, and a general attitude of submissiveness.

This life position is harder to respond to effectively than the last one. But the coach needs to take every opportunity, however small, to learn from the coachee. And given that the coachee must be the 'expert' in her own life (she knows far more about herself than the coach ever can), there should be many such opportunities.

'I'm not OK, you're not OK'

Sometimes people operating from this life position are called cynical. Because their view is that all people are fundamentally out for themselves and are not very admirable or even competent, such individuals are likely to manipulate rather than negotiate, and to assume relationships are dishonest. They sometimes use humour to avoid real engagement with others – the kind of humour that is described as 'always good for a laugh'.

Building a good coaching relationship with someone who operates from this life position is tremendously hard work. The coach is likely to feel their suspiciousness of his motives and competence, without those suspicions ever being expressed openly in a way that could lead to a useful if difficult conversation.

All the coach can do is to plod on, behaving in accordance with his own values and treating the coachee with respect and commitment in exactly the same way he would any other coachee. Sometimes this will move the coachee to a different position, at least in relation to the coach, and then the coaching can begin in earnest.

Sometimes coaching simply cannot work. It is after all a process predicated on the notion that one human being can be completely positively intended towards another. So if a coachee is irrevocably wedded to the contrary view, little progress can be made. In my experience, few people are so irrevocably wedded.

In fact, all of us move in and out of these life positions all the time. In many ways it is a key job of the coach to monitor that movement, and to help the coachee regain 'I'm OK, you're OK' when she has slipped into a defensive place.

> *All the coach can do is to plod on, behaving in accordance with his own values and treating the coachee with respect and commitment in exactly the same way he would any other coachee.*

Mike Brearley describes a time in his life when he was offered insightful coaching by one of the legendary figures in cricket, Wally Hammond. He paid no attention, because at the time he was temporarily in the 'I'm not OK, you're not OK' frame of mind. Here is Mike's story in his own words.

'At 22, I was selected as a young hopeful for the MCC tour of South Africa. Our batting included Boycott, Barber, Dexter, Barrington MJK Smith, and Parfitt. I was there for the experience, most likely. And I did reasonably well until the tests started. Then I was, completely correctly, left out, and left to get on with things in the nets. I was bored. But worse than this, like my father, I was stubborn. I was also ignorant.

'One day at Durban, a sallow man who seemed then very old to me (he was 63), wearing a brown trilby hat (or this is how my memory has it), who had been standing behind the nets watching me bat against David Brown and Robin Hobbs, politely introduced himself, and asked if he could have a word with me. My arms and hands, he said, were too tense. Especially the left arm.

'I was, on the surface, polite. But I didn't really believe him. I went on as before, and became less and less effective. The chances on tour became rarer, and often I would only have one innings in a week or even a fortnight. I gradually became a liability, and my confidence by the end of the tour was rock bottom.

'Now, the man who had offered the advice was none other than Wally Hammond, one of the greatest batsmen ever, who was at that point dying of cancer. This I think was my lowest point, or my most arrogant point.

'In fact, it was only years later that I finally took this important piece of coaching in.

'My question is: why did it take so long to allow this simple, but vital, point house-room in my mind? Why should I have been so arrogant, or suspicious? These are big questions. One thing I have learned as a result. I can't take it for granted that when I ask someone to take something in now, he will be altogether different from me.'

The way in which the 'I'm not OK, you're not OK' frame of mind throws up barriers to coaching is also illustrated well by a story from Adrian Moorhouse's early career as a competitive swimmer.

In swimming coaching, swimmers are coached in groups although they compete as individuals. Coaching by the professional coach would take place one-to-one with each swimmer, but in between times swimmers would progress best if they helped each other as well as practised independently.

Of course, Adrian, as a breast stroke swimmer, would ultimately be competing against the other breast stroke swimmers in his coaching 'squad'. But while training, the best thing for all of them was to coach and support each other, and engage in 'healthy competition' rather than exclusive competitiveness. This is not always easy for people to do, and requires a certain level of maturity and 'OK-ness'.

There were four breast stroke swimmers in Adrian's squad. Three coped well with the set-up, but one couldn't cope at all. He became iso-

photo: Getty Images

Adrian Moorhouse wins gold in the 100 metres breaststroke at the 1988 Seoul Olympics

lated, unable to learn from his colleagues and competitors, and left the squad.

The professional coaches treated all the swimmers the same. But one of them was at that time operating from a life position that meant he could not benefit from the coaching regime. It elicited too much anxiety and destructive competitiveness in him. Within the context of squad coaching, the coaches were unable to support him in moving to the 'I'm OK, you're OK' position.

Our exploration of how coaching looks from the coachee's perspective has led us to clear evidence that what is going on inside the coachee can determine the 'success' or 'failure' of coaching, irrespective of how excellent and apt the coach's advice is, or how well-intentioned the coach. As Adrian puts it, 'when we are coaching, we are always coaching someone's self-belief'.

PART TWO

THE COACH

Introduction

The main instrument of coaching is the coach. While there are numerous frameworks, tools and techniques for coaching (many of which are covered in Part Four of this book), the efficacy of these will always be determined by the way in which they are used. And that is down to the coach.

So, in this part, we look at what makes people good and not so good at coaching. We look below the surface, at beliefs, values and motives, as well as above the surface, at skills, habits and actions. We do not represent a single kind of person, a 'natural' coach, but rather explore the different kinds of people who can coach well, and where their different styles work best.

This part of the book will help coaches recognise their strengths and their weak points, and develop even more capability. It will also help coachees know what to look for when they are choosing a coach. And it will help the managers and HR professionals who are required to 'broker' coaching on behalf of their colleagues to assess and select good coaches. You could very easily design an interview for coaches on the basis of what we present here.

Chapter 4

Beliefs and values

Introduction

What beliefs and values underpin coaching? What are the practical consequences for the success of coaching of different values and beliefs? To what extent do coaches have to subscribe to a particular set of values and beliefs? How can coaches develop the values and beliefs that will be most helpful to them and their coachees? In this chapter we identify a 'core' of values and beliefs essential to good coaching, and also explore the diversity around that core.

Why beliefs and values matter

Human beings are experts at detecting the intentions of other human beings. As social animals, whose survival has always depended on how we get along with others of our kind, we have had to develop the ability to read our fellows. And as animals who, for a long time in our evolutionary history, were the 'most at risk on the savannah' (Winston 2003), we have had to develop very finely tuned sensitivity to anything that might constitute a threat.

So we are good at sensing the underlying motivations of those we come into contact with. We do not always, or even often, do so consciously. We may not think, explicitly, 'that person means me well' or 'that person might do me harm'. But we sense it nonetheless. We may feel uncomfortable, inclined to keep our distance, uneasy. At an unconscious level, we are picking up slight cues that suggest the person we are with is not completely safe.

I am not talking here about extreme or physical danger. I am talking about, for example, the danger that someone may hurt our feelings, or put his own interests before our own. These are the modern equivalents of being left unwarned about a predator on the savannah.

In a coaching relationship, it is important for the coachee to feel safe with the coach. If she doesn't, a large part of her energy and attention will be diverted into protecting herself, and away from developing and growing. The people who are best at making others feel safe are people whose intentions towards them are not only benign but actively positive. They are people who not only don't mean others harm, they mean others well, and are intent on doing something about it.

And our intentions towards others are determined by our beliefs and values. They run deep; they are not collections of tools and techniques; they are at the core of who we want to be and of what we consider matters. And because human beings have such excellent 'intent detectors', it is not enough for a coach to behave *as if* she had positive intent.

> For a coach to create the safe environment the best coaching requires, she must hold the beliefs and values that guarantee the coachee her positive intent.

At some level, albeit often unconscious, her coachee will sense there is no substance behind the behaviour. No, for a coach to create the safe environment the best coaching requires, she must hold the beliefs and values that guarantee the coachee her positive intent.

Beliefs and values that help and hinder

What beliefs and values are these? Probably the most important, and the foundation stone of effective coaching, is 'respect'. By respect, I mean the belief that every human being sees the world differently, and has his own good reasons for seeing it the way he does. No other human being has the right to impose his way of seeing the world on another, nor to deny the sense it makes to the person who holds it.

(Of course, this does not mean a belief that everyone can act according to their own individual view of the world. Actions have to be controlled and governed in the light of their impact on others. But the view of the world that led to the actions is to be respected: recognised for what it is, understood in terms of where it came from, and left to be determined by the individual who holds it.)

Let's just make this 'respect' tangible with an example from a coaching context. Suppose a coachee says 'bosses are always out for themselves; I don't trust them, and I don't like lining their pockets'. A coach who believes in respect is likely to explore this view of the world, trying to understand exactly what it means and how it came about. She may comment on its being a fairly extreme view. She will want to understand what consequences this view of the world has for the coachee, and how fixed and universal it is. The coachee will be able to explore all this thoroughly with his coach, and may come to understand some new things as a result, which may lead him to moderate his view, or to plan action to protect against undesired consequences of that view.

A coach who doesn't believe in respect as I am defining it is likely to tell the coachee he is wrong. Immediately the coachee is diminished. The coach has judged him according to her own view of the world. It has become less safe to be with this coach.

Also, if you don't value respect as I have defined it, you will be at risk of trying to impose your view on your coachee. This runs counter to one of the key goals of coaching: to increase the range of choices open to the coachee.

Another belief a coach needs to have is that people can change, that they can improve their lives and that they can fulfil more of their potential. It is hard to imagine how a coach who didn't have this basically optimistic view of human possibility could create a positive environment for his coachee. The coachee would sense a mismatch between what the coach was saying, and what he was really thinking. That mismatch would make her uneasy, and less safe.

I am not suggesting here that coaches need to be, or even should be, facile optimists, 'Pollyannas' of organisational life. A coach who doesn't understand how difficult and intractable many of a coachee's issues are will not be much help. Also, a coach who is not prepared to say 'I just can't see a way forward for you on this one' or 'you are in an impossible situation', and share the coachee's sense of frustration and impotence, is likely to seem out of touch with the coachee's world.

But what the coach does need to believe is that the coachee can find a way through. He needs to believe that people are more resourceful than they know, that given the right support they can work out what to do, and that adults as well as children have an instinct towards growth and development.

If a coach detects she is losing her confidence in people's ability to develop she needs to address that as a matter of urgency. It may happen because of events in her own life; it may happen because of a coaching assignment that has hit a brick wall. She may need some coaching herself to rekindle that essential optimism about others.

Respect, and optimism about people, are in my view the most important beliefs and values a coach needs, for her coachees to feel safe and at ease in the coaching relationship. Other beliefs and values that are important include the belief that individuals matter and can make a difference, valuing trial and error at least as much as perfection (it's the journey that matters as much as the arrival), and the value of personal integrity.

This last is about being consistent and transparent in the way we behave, so that others can see clearly who we are and where we are coming from. This is something else coachees need from coaches in order to feel safe, and so free to work on their own issues.

So there are some general beliefs and values that are particularly necessary for a coach to have. In addition, all of our many and diverse, specific and interconnected beliefs and values are likely to be relevant to the way we work as coaches, and to have a profound impact on our strengths and weaknesses in that role. More than anything else, it is beliefs and values that determine which kinds of coaching assignments coaches are best suited to. For example:

- Do we believe that belonging to an organisation necessarily involves an individual in compromise and some pain? Do we believe that organisations are a 'necessary evil'? We may be well suited to coaching people who are suffering because of organisational pressures and requirements. They will sense in us a recognition of their pain, an understanding that it is not 'their fault', combined with a belief that they can and will get through it.
- Do we believe passionately in the importance of a balanced life? We may be well suited to people whose work is threatening to overwhelm them.
- Do we value youth and see the innovation and challenges youth brings as invaluable to society? Then we may be well suited to work with 'high fliers' and new graduates.

If we are trying to be the best coaches we can be, we should reflect constantly on what our beliefs and values are. The more aware of them we are, the better we shall understand where our coaching is naturally effective and where it is not. If we are choosing a coach for ourselves or for someone else, we should explore their beliefs and values so that we know not only if these are broadly appropriate but also whether they fit the coaching assignment.

Beliefs and values are about prioritisation. Sure, we all want world peace and self-fulfilment. But where is our limited energy focused? Is it focused on helping the disadvantaged? Or on harnessing the best creativity and talent? The way to understand what is really important to us is to force ourselves to make choices. Good questions are 'what are the five things I believe most passionately?' and 'when have I made personal sacrifices because of something I believed in?' and 'what would my friends say matters most to me?'

Beware a coach who claims to care about everything. She probably doesn't care much about anything.

Building helpful beliefs and values

Of course, it is true that many of our underlying beliefs and values are determined by our experience as children, by what we saw in our parents, and by the patterns of family relationships we were part of. I continue to be amazed at the strength of these influences, which of course are well documented throughout the psychological literature.

Just recently, for example, I came across a banker who couldn't give polished, confident presentations. Also, he was such a teamplayer that he sometimes didn't put his own view across strongly enough. As I talked to him, his absolute distaste for anything that smacked of self-promotion at others' expense became clear.

When we tracked this underlying value system (against individualism, for the team) back to its roots, he realised that it began when as a child he observed how his whole family had to adapt to the wants and needs of its most dominant member: his father. He saw his mother, to whom he was close, suffer in consequence, and in that childhood was laid down the rejection of individualism that was now causing him some problems as a senior manager. (Needless to say, his team ethic was also the source of much of his success.)

But even though our beliefs and values have such deep roots, that does not mean we cannot strengthen particular ones or even develop new ones. We can do it by focusing our attention in a particular direction, and by exposing ourselves to particular people and situations. I remember a policeman friend of mine, who said one of the things he disliked most about his job was that it encouraged him to be cynical about people. Day after day, he saw people in their worst light.

So if we want to develop optimism, we need to do the reverse of the policeman. We need to focus on people's achievements and capacity for development. When we hear of someone who has triumphed in the face of adversity, we need to find out more. We need to read about mountaineers, doctors, adventurers, explorers; we need to engage in conversations with as many people as possible about the things they are most proud of having achieved, about great mistakes and setbacks and how they recovered, about hopes and aspirations and what they are doing to achieve them.

If we want to develop respect, we need to expose ourselves to as great a diversity of perspective in others as possible, and to focus on seeing how different ways of viewing the world work (rather than on how they fail to work). Time spent living and working with people from other cultures builds respect. So does friendship with a wide range of people, from different backgrounds and walks of life. We should pay attention to outcomes that surprise us (in other words, outcomes that contradict our own world view and encourage us to be more respectful of others'). Coachees who succeed in a different way from how we as coaches could ever have imagined them doing so are invaluable teachers of respect.

In many ways, being a coach is an extreme exercise in developing respect and optimism. If we do it right, it will encourage in us just those beliefs and values that are likely to make us most effective. It will set up a virtuous circle as a result of which we as coaches are enhanced. And so we are led

If we want to develop respect, we need to expose ourselves to as great a diversity of perspective in others as possible, and to focus on seeing how different ways of viewing the world work (rather than on how they fail to work).

naturally to the issue of the coach's motives for coaching, the subject matter of our next chapter.

Chapter 5

Motives

Introduction

If people are expert at detecting the intent of others, then the motives of coaches are as important as their beliefs and values. (Indeed, motives are likely to be intimately connected with beliefs and values.) There is a view, with which I have a considerable degree of sympathy, that intent is all that matters. In fact, it is also necessary, to be a good coach, to have certain skills and habits. But if the coach has excellent technique and inappropriate motives, the coachee is likely to feel unsafe, and rightly so.

Coaching should not be manipulative. Manipulation reduces the power and autonomy of the person being manipulated. Coaching is aimed at achieving the opposite: an increase in power and autonomy. So let us examine good and bad motives for coaching, and how they affect what happens.

A desire to do something for the future

Often people are drawn towards coaching when they are nearing the end of their time in organisational life. They begin to ask themselves questions related to 'legacy' – what shall I be leaving behind me for the next generation? They come to the view that the best use they can make of their experience and accumulated wisdom is to coach those who are still 'young' in organisational terms. They want to feel they have made a difference, and they reckon that helping others to achieve their potential, which will have long-lasting impact, is a good way of doing so.

I had a coachee who was one of the best global account managers in his organisation. He had won and maintained business worth many hundreds of thousands for his organisation. Now in his mid-fifties, he recognised that he was probably not going to rise much higher, and also that his energy to win and run the business, all over the world, was lessening. A colleague of his suggested he should concentrate on coaching the younger account managers. He should begin to teach, not just do.

This desire to do something for the future is not limited to older people. But it is typical of that stage of life, where our own powers are declining and yet we still want to make a significant contribution.

As a motive for coaching, it has these benefits. The coachee need not feel threatened by her coach's own ambitions. She may feel nurtured by the 'elder relative' dynamic. The very fact of being chosen as a coachee by someone who has such a motivation affirms her own future prospects. It could make her feel even more strongly that she has potential, and be even more determined to fulfil it. Also, it may be reassuring to her to be coached by someone who has been so successful himself.

This motive can mean trouble for the coaching relationship, however. It can easily result in a desire on the part of the coach to sell his own recipes for success. These may get in the way of those that will work for the coachee. Also, the coach may be out of date (this is not a problem unless the coach has a strong view he wants to push; you don't need to be up to date to help a coachee explore and understand things for herself; in fact, sometimes being out of date yourself as coach is helpful!).

Finally, the coach may, unconsciously, be looking to live vicariously through the coachee. While all coaches derive huge amounts of pleasure from the successes of people they coach, it is a different matter when they start to feel about that success as if it were their own. The coachee will find such vicarious living intrusive, and stifling. Coaches need to be happy to be coaches, not still hankering after being excellent themselves at what their coachee is good at.

I remember talking to a senior investment banker who wanted a coach and had been sent a number of candidates by his HR manager. They were all ex-senior investment bankers (as well as experienced coaches, needless to say). My friend rejected them all. He said they were 'a bunch of old City bores'. He said that the financial environment was changing so rapidly the knowledge of yesterday was already irrelevant.

I think he must have sensed that they would try to peddle their own expertise, instead of help him develop his.

A desire to learn

Perhaps you are surprised to see this heading. You may have expected 'a desire to teach'. But in my experience many of the best coaches come to coaching because of their love of learning. I mean 'learning' in its broadest sense here – changing, developing, finding out new things, being surprised, following one's curiosity. Such coaches feel at their most alive when learning is going on, their own and other people's.

So they are drawn to coaching because the coachee is explicitly out to learn, and because they know they will learn too. They will learn about another person's world and challenges. They will, hopefully, learn how best to help and support this individual (coaching assignments never follow a recipe; every coachee is different). They will have their own beliefs and ideas challenged as they work with the coachee to find paths through difficult and complex issues.

Maybe this sounds too selfish. Surely the coach should be entirely focused on the coachee's learning? It might be very nice for her to learn too, but it's hardly the main point.

Yet the interesting thing is, the more the coach is learning, the more likely it is that the coachee is. Learning is infectious. It is the coach's desire to understand – to learn – that leads her to ask lots of probing questions. In answering them, the coachee learns too. Also, the coachee can 'catch' from the coach a curious and exploratory frame of mind, through that well-documented form of social learning, 'modelling'. We tend to imitate the behaviour of people who are important to us.

So in many ways the coach is more helpful to her coachees when he focuses on learning, not on teaching.

A desire to connect

Many coaches are very sociable, warm people. One of their primary motivations is to connect with others, to move beyond the social niceties to a relationship where openness and mutual understanding is possible. Those kinds of relationships are deeply affirming.

The benefits to the coachee of this motive on the part of the coach is the warmth and the humanity of the relationship within which coaching occurs. The connection will mean that coach and coachee get to know each other as people fairly quickly; the coachee then feels comfortable, and – that favourite word of mine – safe.

Where this kind of motive can cause problems is if the coach starts looking for friendship first, and the chance to do a good coaching job second. Most coaching includes some element of confrontation, of challenge. If the coach is too 'pally' with the coachee, then he may not be able to do this. (That is in part why, although we can get coaching from our friends, coaching is different from friendship: it has different priorities.) Also, once the coaching relationship has become more about satisfying the coach's needs for friendship than the coachee's need to grow, the coach will start to make choices that are not in the best interests of the coachee.

Finally, we need to remember that coachees do not always want to connect with their coaches on a level of warmth and intimacy. I can easily identify many coachees of mine who have preferred a slightly formal relationship. They see the formality as evidence of objectivity and professionalism. They would be made unnecessarily uneasy by too much friendliness. Of course, they do not want any sense of hostility. But they need a detached yet positively intended mind to work with them on their issues.

A desire to help

The desire to help others is a fundamental human motive, although it is stronger in some than in others. In some people, it takes the extreme form of living a life of service, as a doctor in a Third World country, for example. At the other end of the spectrum are people who have little desire to help anyone outside their own immediate family.

All coaches are probably motivated to some extent by a desire to help. They feel more worthwhile if they can contribute to others' success and well-being. Within bounds, this motive is helpful to coaching.

It becomes problematic when it is so strong that it begins to lead to a desire to control. Occasionally a coach will become convinced she knows what is best for her coachee. She needs to be able to make her view available to her coachee, without persuading him to accept it. There is a fine line between saying what you think, and telling someone what to think. A desire to help that is too strong can push us from the former to the latter. The desire to help in the short term (which is all we can ever see) must be tempered by the desire to build the coachee's long-term capability and power to achieve what he wants.

The coachee should not be burdened by the coach's desire to help. I had a coachee once who found it too painful to see me because she wasn't making any progress. I hope I wasn't guilty of pressurising her with my desire to help, but maybe I was.

Too much helping fosters dependency. A colleague of mine had a succession of 'life' and 'career' coaches. Sometimes, he would be seeing two contemporaneously! Over many years, his problems remained the same. From what I could tell, the coaches were doing their best to be helpful, and sometimes when he told me what they had said I would think they had hit the nail on the head. But nothing changed.

Then he heard of a new coach, someone he really wanted to work with. He had an excellent reputation. He went for his first session, and came back furious. The coach had refused to take him on! He said that my colleague had already had so much coaching, it was unlikely any more would be worthwhile. Within two weeks of that meeting, my colleague made some of the fundamental changes other coaches had been counselling for years.

Now I'm not saying that the last coach wasn't motivated by a desire to help. But he knew when to rein it back — and paradoxically ended up helping my colleague even more.

Connected with a desire to help is a desire to do something useful. This motive is different though because it focuses on a broader context than just on the individual.

A colleague of mine, a very skilled and humanistic coach, once described his purpose in coaching as 'to get the person back to work'. He observes how people can find themselves at odds with their roles, unable at that moment to engage fully in work that is meaningful to them and productive for the organisation. (Typical scenarios are a falling-out with the boss, a disappointment such as a failure to get promoted, or a change in role that doesn't fit well the individual's wants and capabilities.)

People in such situations are 'stalled' because their relationship with their work has temporarily broken down. They need to sort the relationship out before they can get on with the work. My colleague sees coaching as an important way of helping an individual do just that. Not only can she then get on with her work, but she can also get on with her life (of which work is for most of us an important part). And the organisation can get on with its work. This motivation of my colleague's is an example of a desire to do something useful.

> A colleague of mine, a very skilled and humanistic coach, once described his purpose in coaching as 'to get the person back to work'. He observes how people can find themselves at odds with their roles, unable at that moment to engage fully in work that is meaningful to them and productive for the organisation.

A coach's desire to do something useful is generally helpful to coaching. It is not selfish or egotistical; it provides a framework of meaningfulness for the coach without focusing on the coach's personal needs. Of course, the coach needs to look at what he considers useful. This will be dictated to a large extent by his beliefs and values. My colleague referred to above, for example, has a belief (which I share) that people's lives are enhanced by doing meaningful work.

A desire to preach

This is an inappropriate motive for a coach. If a coach has a very strong view – about how people should behave, about how a job should be done, about how to be happy – and is motivated to coach because that is a means of spreading her philosophy, then that coach will not be well placed to work with the coachee towards the achievement of his goals. Her own agenda will take priority.

That breaks one of the fundamental principles of coaching, namely that the coachee is the centre and the focus of coaching. It also breaks a second principle, that the coach should work to increase the range of choices the coachee has.

There is nothing wrong with wanting to put across a specific message. It's just that coaching is not the way to do it.

A desire to be rewarded

Some coaches are motivated by a desire for recognition. Some coaches do it simply as a way to make money. Some do it because the organisation guarantees them rewards if they undertake more coaching: promotion, a bonus, a salary rise.

As for most activities that depend on building a meaningful relationship, these kinds of instrumental motives don't work well. How could you honestly say to a coachee: 'I am coaching you in order to earn some money now I am retired?' Or: 'I am coaching you because I have to demonstrate competence in coaching before I can be promoted to a management grade?'

Of course, such motives may lie behind an initial interest in coaching, and may still be around when the coaching relationship starts. We all have to earn a living; we all strive for success. But unless some motivation of more relevance to the needs and hopes of the coachee takes precedence, the coaching will be at best formulaic, at worst exploitative. Coaching needs to have some passion in it, and that passion needs to be about the coachee: her possibilities, her future, her hopes and dreams.

The coach needs to know how he will answer the question 'Why are you coaching me?' He may never be asked it, but nonetheless his answer will probably be the single most important determinant of the success of the coaching.

The organisation's motives

Most coaching takes place in an organisational context. The organisation has commissioned and paid for it. And the organisation will have its reasons for doing so. Coaching is not cheap. Bought from an external provider, it is probably the single most expensive form of development in terms of pounds per development hour per manager. Organised as an internal management responsibility, again it is expensive.

Managers will need to spend time one-to-one with their people, over and above the time they already spend on planning, reviewing, appraising. True, it may save time in the long term. It is intended to raise the capability of people at all levels, and to increase their self-reliance and willingness to take responsibility. But these are the ultimate benefits. In the short term, it has to be paid for.

So why do organisations do it, and what is the impact of the organisation's motives on the coach's motives, and on the 'psychological contract' between coach and coachee?

The best organisational motive from this point of view is the motive to support employees to realise their full potential. Where there is understanding of and commitment to the view that the organisation's long-term success depends on the skill, development and morale of its people, and where coaching is seen as a key element in the strategy for achieving high levels of skill, quality development and good morale, then the organisation's motivation positions the coach well.

It will sit comfortably with her own motivations to build something for the future, to learn and to connect. The coachee will feel that the psychological contract is clear and benign: you will support me in becoming the best I can be, and as a consequence through my work I shall bring increasing value to my organisation.

Mostly, though, organisational motives – just like individual ones – are much more mixed. Sometimes organisations want particular problems to be 'fixed'. More times than I can count, I have been contacted by an organisation which has a 'problem' with one of its senior managers. He loses his temper and shouts at staff; he goes behind his colleagues' back and undermines them; he isn't bringing in enough business. The examples are legion. The organisation (often as represented by the individual's boss and HR manager) hopes a programme of coaching will 'sort this individual out'.

This does not fit so comfortably with the motives a coach needs to have. The requirement to 'fix' something jars with the coach's reluctance to 'preach' or 'control'. It ties her hands from the start. The organisation is trying to set up the psychological contract with the coachee: we shall pay for you to have coaching, and as a consequence you will behave more appropriately. The coach will need to negotiate sufficient space around her coaching to allow her to develop a separate psychological contract that is more appropriate, something along the lines of: 'I shall explore with you what is causing you problems in your role, and as a consequence you will identify what you need to do differently.'

Negotiating that space can be very difficult. I refused a coaching assignment because an organisation wanted regular progress reports on the coachee from me, for example. And sometimes an organisation will sack a coach because he is not delivering the 'results' they want.

Sometimes organisations pay lip-service to coaching. They know that they will be more attractive to potential recruits if they are seen as 'coaching organisations'. They may want to cultivate a particular image in the market place. But there is no real depth of commitment to people's development. They are akin to the coach who is only motivated by recognition or money. Again, it will be hard for coaches to establish their own integrity against such a cynical backdrop. It will be harder for internal coaches than external ones, but even external ones are likely to be less effective as a result of the organisation's unhelpful motivation.

Sometimes organisations offer coaching because they are hoping to retain people, or to get rid of them. They may offer coaching as a perk to those they value, or as a warning signal to those they don't. When the coaching relationship begins with such an exercise of power by the organisation it is much harder for the coach to develop a sense of powerfulness in the coachee.

Coaching happens in the privacy of a one-to-one relationship, bounded by strict rules of confidentiality. But it does not happen in a vacuum. The organisation's pressures, drivers and culture will impact on its effectiveness. Coaches need to understand the motives of their paymasters. But they need to make clear that coaching has its own sets of requirements and dynamics. They cannot work to the organisation's agenda where the organisation's agenda is in conflict with that of the individual. That is a function of management, not of coaching.

Chapter 6

Skills

Introduction

In this chapter we look at the skilful behaviours of a good coach. Skills can be learned, although not everyone can learn them. People learn best and most easily those skills that are consistent with their beliefs, values and motives.

A long time ago, I worked with 'underachieving' teenagers in an inner city school. My job was to teach them the skills of reading, writing and arithmetic. There is no doubt they could have learned them. They had learned easily how to mend motorbikes, and drive, both things I was struggling with at the time. They were sophisticated in their arguments and knowledgeable about many things. But they were slow at learning the things I was teaching them, and never learned them very well. You can readily appreciate how little connection there was between what mattered to them and the skills I was trying to teach them.

I had an experience that reminded me of this a couple of years ago. The MD of an estate agency asked me to coach him in listening skills. Suffice it to say, 360-feedback suggested he learned little from me! But he was a man who believed passionately in a particular kind of selling; his success was founded on his ability to put himself about, to make an impression, to carry people away with the force of his own certainty and enthusiasm. Also, he believed that to be successful you have to move fast. How could listening skills be his forte?

(I wouldn't like you to think I gave up. He solved the problem by getting his second-in-command, a much more measured and less ebullient personality, to do his listening for him and to communicate other people's key messages to the MD in a very forceful, concise way.)

So the skills of coaching are not independent of values, beliefs and motives. I don't think you can be a good listener if you're not interested in what someone is saying. Nonetheless we need to be clear about the skills a good coach needs. Positive intent is necessary, but not sufficient.

Active listening

In my view, this is the single most important skill for a coach. It is what enables the coach to understand the coachee and her world. Every other intervention the coach makes has to be based on that under-standing, and the more complete that understanding is, the more effec-tively the coach will intervene.

This kind of listening is called 'active' for a number of reasons, and these reasons give us important insight into what it is about.

- First, it is active because the listener is doing things. We shall talk in more depth about what she is doing.
- Second, it is active because while it is going on, changes are hap-pening. The person being listened to is seeing things in new ways and starting to feel differently about things. A different kind of relationship is being formed between listener and speaker. Active lis-tening causes things to happen. It is a positive act, not a passive time preceding the 'real action'. Sometimes active listening achieves the goal of coaching all by itself.
- Third, it is 'active' because it takes effort and application to do well. People who learn how to do it often say it is more tiring than any-thing else they do. Passive listening often feels like taking a rest. Active listening never does. It is work, and hard work at that.

Probably the greatest active listener of all time was Carl Rogers, the psychotherapist. He believed that many of us suffer unhappiness and loss of purpose because we experienced insufficient 'unconditional positive regard' when we were growing up. That is, the sense that we are loved and respected for who we are; and that the love and respect we receive are not contingent on our behaving in order to please others.

Rogers believed that giving adults some hefty doses of 'uncondi-tional positive regard' could help to put this right, increasing their sense of self-worth and their ability to take positive action to achieve their goals. (You can see the connection with the purposes of coach-ing.) Rogers demonstrated unconditional positive regard through active listening.

What did he do? He focused his attention completely on the person he was listening to. You can see when someone is deeply attentive in that way. They lean forward when the speaker is speak-ing intensely; they lean back when the speaker is more reflective.

They nod and make nonverbal utterances – 'uh huh', 'yeah', 'mmm', 'I see', for example – in response to the speaker's points. They notice not only what the speaker is saying but how he is saying it. They notice changes in his voice, his body posture, his skin colour, his eyes.

They notice changes in themselves that happen in response to changes in the speaker. They find themselves feeling a sense of anticipation as the speaker builds his story to a climax, sorrow as the speaker tells of disappointment; they laugh with the speaker, and often their own behaviour will unintentionally 'mirror' that of the speaker. Their entire attention, both conscious and unconscious, is focused on the speaker.

This has two profound effects. First, the speaker has a sense of being attended to in a way that he will rarely experience. He will attend more closely to his own words as a consequence. He will learn things about his own story. He will 'realise what he is saying' and what it means to him.

Second, the listener will receive a vast amount of data about the speaker. Her understanding of him will be far deeper and more comprehensive than if she had just listened to his words, and had simultaneously been thinking about what she planned to say next.

The reason why active listening is such hard work is that we are not used to focusing our attention so entirely. Typically we will be attending to a whole range of things simultaneously: the words we are hearing, our own thought about those words, what our next words will be, and some random things like what we are planning to have for dinner or some anger at someone that is still unresolved. That is normal listening, and most of the time it does fine. But a coach has to practise active listening.

Carl Rogers did more, as a consequence of being entirely focused on hearing another person's story. Sometimes he would simply repeat what the speaker had said. Speaker: 'I was really disappointed.' Rogers: 'You were really disappointed.'

These repetitions happened because Rogers recognised that these were key parts of the speaker's story, that they had special emphasis and poignancy. He was moved to repeat them.

Sometimes he would paraphrase: 'I'm hearing you say you were at a loss at this point – is that right?' He did this because he wanted to be sure he had understood something that he sensed was important. The speaker might say 'Yes, that's it'. Or he might say 'No not quite' and put the listener right. Either way, Rogers would understand the speaker better.

Rogers would also do things to help the speaker keep going. He would convey that he wasn't judging the speaker negatively with comments such as 'I've seen that happen many times' or 'that's understandable' or 'I've done the same myself'. When people are talking about something personal, they can stall through a fear that the listener is thinking badly of them. Rogers was not, and he showed it.

Active listeners can help the speaker when he loses his thread. 'Where was I?' 'You were just explaining how the promotion system works here.' 'Oh yes...'

So these are the signs of active listening. You can develop your skill somewhat by practising the behaviours. But you will develop your skill more by learning how to become deeply interested in another person. The most effective way to do this, unsurprisingly, is by finding a link between a deep interest in the person and a belief or value of your own.

For example, suppose you value diversity. Then you can make the link that it is only by stepping fully into another person's shoes and experiencing the world as they do that you will really show respect for diversity. The link is made; the interest will follow; and so will the active listening behaviours.

Suppose, like the colleague of mine I mentioned in the chapter on 'Motives', you want to 'get people back to work'. You won't be able to do that unless you fully understand the barriers. You will only get that understanding from the individual herself. And so your interest in her story is kindled.

When you find your attention wandering, as it will, you should remind yourself of why this information contained in your coachee's story and in the way he tells it is so important to you. Also, if you look for an opportunity to do one of the more active things (reflecting back, paraphrasing or sharing a common experience) that will help you re-focus your attention. Sometimes taking a note or two helps too, but be careful not to let that break the connection between you and your coachee. You will probably need to explain why you take notes, either at the outset, or when you realise you need to do it.

Questioning

Questioning is the second most important skill, and together with active listening probably achieves 80 per cent of the positive outcome of coaching. In Part Four we provide some specific questioning sequences that can be helpful at different times in coaching. Here we shall look more broadly at what it means to say a coach has 'good questioning skills'.

First, such a coach will ask questions that get the coachee thinking in new ways. They will often be questions the coachee has never been asked, or asked himself, before. Typically, such questions elicit the response 'That's a good question!' and a reflective pause.

Where do such questions come from? (You can't list them, provide a resource pack of 'good questions for coaches', because what makes a question good is specific to the issue and the person.) Good questions come, just like active listening, from a deep interest on the part of the coach in the coachee's experience of the world. But the coach is more detached from that experience of the world than the coachee. So when her detachment combines with her curiosity it leads her to ask new questions that may get at the heart of what's going on.

Here is an example from a recent coaching session with a senior accountant. He was struggling with the huge workload his new management role entailed and with the fact that his secretary, who had worked for him for many years and with whom he had a good relationship, had not been able to respond to the new demands on her of her boss's new role. Unintentionally, she was contributing to his problems. He was under pressure to fire her (from well-meaning colleagues) but was caught up in feelings of guilt and also anger: why were his colleagues pushing him towards a course of action so at odds with his own values, and about a matter that was his business only?

His coach asked him: 'How is your secretary feeling about her new responsibilities?' The accountant stopped short. 'You know, I never asked her. I don't know.' That was a good question. The coachee saw he only had part of the information he needed to decide what to do. The question unblocked him.

> Good questions come, just like active listening, from a deep interest on the part of the coach in the coachee's experience of the world.

It wasn't a subtle or sophisticated question. But the coach was intently interested in understanding the problem, and yet not caught up in the feelings that the coachee had; she just saw there was some important information she hadn't heard yet. The coachee's feelings of guilt and anger led him to focus on his own shortcomings and responsibilities; the coach's question reminded him that another person's views and responsibilities were also important.

If the coach is interested in getting the whole picture, she will ask good questions, questions that help the coachee get a fuller picture.

The coach will also ask 'good' questions when she taps into her own different view of the world to extend and enhance the coachee's view of the world. Probably the best-known example of such a question is this one: 'How do you feel about that?' In the coach's view of the world, feelings are important and a legitimate topic of discussion. They dictate what people will do, far more often than logic, and they are certainly key to a coachee's ability to achieve difficult goals.

In the world of many coachees, feelings are ignored; they are embarrassing to talk about, even seen as inappropriate to talk about. By asking a question about feelings, the coach is making available to the coachee a whole extra source of information he might never spontaneously access for himself.

Other good questions of this kind include questions about what coachees hope for, about what they are most proud of, and about their imaginings and fantasies. Of course, a coach has to understand and respect her coachee's world. But she will be more helpful to him if she also stays in her own world and draws on its different sets of principles and norms to cast another light on his.

> *In the coach's view of the world, feelings are important and a legitimate topic of discussion. They dictate what people will do, far more often than logic, and they are certainly key to a coachee's ability to achieve difficult goals.*

Another sign of skilful questioning is that the questions flow naturally from the dialogue. This is the difference between a series of skilful questions and an interrogation. In this way, the coachee leads the conversation as much as does the coach. Although there may be times when the coach decides to use a particular sequence of questions to achieve a particular purpose (see Part Four), for the most part the coach is taking her cue from something the coachee has chosen to say.

The variety of different question types also marks out the skilful coach. These range from very open questions, which give the coachee almost total freedom to say what is on his mind (such as, 'what's been happening?' at the start of a session) to probing questions, which have the precision of a scalpel, helping the coach and coachee understand something important in all its complexity ('what did you do?' 'how did they respond?' 'what happened next?' 'where exactly were you standing just then?'). The coach may ask questions that have a 'yes' or 'no' answer to help the coachee get clarity or commit to a view or a decision; she may ask wandering, obscure questions to encourage the coachee to talk about things he is still not clear about.

We develop our questioning skill best by developing our capacity for curiosity. Encourage yourself to wonder, about all kinds of people and all kinds of situations. Ask yourself lots of questions, and you will become better at asking them of other people.

Reframing

As we have seen with skilful questions, one of the ways a coach is helpful is by offering new ways of thinking about old problems. Skill at reframing enables him to do just this.

Reframing is changing the meaning of something by putting it in a different context.

Here is an example. A teenage boy argues with everything his mother says. She puts his arguing into the context of his respect for her. 'He doesn't have any respect for me,' she thinks, and feels angry. Then she talks to a friend about the problem. The friend says 'maybe he's trying to find some independence'. She puts the teenager's behaviour in the context of the difficulties of adolescence. This reframe works for his mother, who now feels compassionate towards her son.

Who knows what it is right for that mother to feel? And who cares? It's better if what she feels has better consequences for her. When she feels angry, the consequences are rows and tensions at home. When she feels compassionate, the consequence is a calmer atmosphere. Now that she has two possible frames to put round her son's behaviour, she has choice about what she feels and what consequences ensue.

Often when we are stuck, a reframe will help us move forward.

A coachee of mine wanted to leave her job but couldn't. She saw it as a secure job, and although she was unhappy in it she was too frightened to leave. She had good benefits and a guaranteed final salary pension. She had worked there for 15 years. Her job meant safety to her. Then one day she couldn't go to work; she had an acute stress reaction and couldn't stop crying. She came to understand the links between her feelings about work and her stress reaction. She began to see her job as threatening her health. It began to mean danger. (Nothing else had changed.) She handed in her notice soon afterwards.

Coaches who are skilful at seeing things from lots of different angles, and at suggesting different ways of seeing things that strike a chord with their coachees can use that skill to unblock their clients. But this is not about prescribing a different way of seeing things. It is not about saying 'You should see this as an opportunity, not a threat' or 'You should see he's just trying to be helpful.' Coachees will choose how they want to see things. What it is about is putting forward possibilities for seeing things differently, one of which may capture the coachee's attention.

I remember working with a group of people who were learning the skill of reframing. They took it in turns to describe an intractable problem that was causing them stress. We had to brainstorm lots of ways of looking at the problem that could reduce the amount of stress it caused the person who had the problem and see if he latched on to one. One of the men said he couldn't stand his brother's wife. He found her unattractive, graceless, and obnoxious. He wished so much his brother had never married her. He felt regretful and frustrated.

Ideas for reframes came thick and fast. 'She's an opportunity to learn tolerance'; 'you can be glad when she leaves'; 'you can use her as a warning to yourself when you're at risk of getting married'. But the reframe that worked for him was 'You will never be jealous of your brother again.' The trainer who came up with this one had noticed the competitiveness that had come across when this man was talking about his brother. He found a reframe that struck a chord.

Reframes that don't speak to people's underlying values, beliefs and motives won't work.

A coachee of mine is very hurt and angry because, contrary to what she feels she was promised, she is not going to make it on to the board of her organisation. Although she is extremely well thought of, and also has by now earned enough never to need to work again, she feels she has failed.

You might imagine I have tried lots of reframes about being liberated from the journey up the greasy pole, being free to run the rest of her career on her own terms, having the opportunity to adjust her perspective on success and failure before she retires, and so on. None of these works for her. She believes status is the most important measure of achievement. We are now trying to change the meaning that status has for her. It won't be easy.

Confronting

Sometimes it is the coach's job to turn up the heat, to generate some emotion that may provide the impetus for change. That's where confronting comes in.

Confronting is bringing to someone's attention, in a way they cannot ignore, some information that they cannot reconcile with their current view of reality. Here is an example.

A coachee says he wants to improve his time management. He is late for every coaching session. The coach says. 'I am wondering about something. You say time management is important to you, that you see it as part of what makes a manager successful. But you are late for every session with me. How can you explain this?'

Here is another example. 'You have told me that everything would be fine if you were working for a different boss. Yet most of the things you describe as frustrations or difficulties are in fact to do with your relationships with your colleagues. I'm puzzled.'

And another. 'How does your wish to be promoted stack up with your lack of respect for authority?'

The coach is not trying to catch the coachee out, or provoke an argument. Nor is she making a sarcastic point (tone of voice is even and factual). She is rather identifying discrepancies, because they may hold the key to why things are as they are. When the discrepancy is resolved, coach and coachee's understanding will move forward and something important may change.

> *Confronting is bringing to someone's attention, in a way they cannot ignore, some information that they cannot reconcile with their current view of reality.*

The coachee who was late for his sessions realised time management is in fact very low on his list of priorities. He was only focusing on it because he'd been told to. He and the coach started work on an issue of much more importance to him.

The coachee who was complaining about his boss was rather upset by the coach's observation. He went quiet for a while, and the session finished early. But at the start of the next session he said he'd been doing some thinking. He'd come to realise that many of his problems were to do with his own competitiveness and jealousy. The coaching began to make more progress.

The coachee who didn't respect authority replied that he wanted to be promoted in order to be a different kind of boss. This resulted in a whole new line of exploration.

Confronting requires courage as well as skill. It is not easy to turn the heat up. Many coaches, and they are not the most effective, avoid confronting. They prefer to stay supportive and affirming throughout. Other coaches confront too readily, often out of impatience. The skill is to identify a mismatch between two things your coachee says, or between what she says and what she does, which seems to you to be at the heart of things.

Then the skill is to point out the mismatch clearly and calmly, and to be puzzled, not judgemental or triumphant. Hold on to your curiosity. Where an intelligent and well-intentioned human being (your coachee) is believing two contradictory things, it probably means there is something important he hasn't understood fully yet. Getting to the bottom of such misunderstandings can be a door to change and growth.

There is another kind of confronting. If your coachee tells you two things that don't stack up, and you point it out, he may come to understand external reality differently and more fully.

I had a coachee who told me she had nothing but positive feedback from her internal clients. They valued her work, and kept her busy. But she also told me that her boss, who was in regular contact with her clients, never had time to see her, and was avoiding formalising her role. She had understandably been dealing with this difficult situation by focusing on doing good work for her clients, and had pushed the boss's behaviour to the back of her mind.

I helped her focus on understanding what these two conflicting messages meant. She came to the view that while people thought she did good work, they weren't prepared to pay for it (she was on her boss's budget, and essentially provided 'free' to the internal clients). I believe that when she was made redundant she was more prepared for it as a consequence.

Confronting requires courage as well as skill. It is not easy to turn the heat up. Many coaches, and they are not the most effective, avoid confronting. They prefer to stay supportive and affirming throughout.

Confronting needs to be done with care and sensitivity, and with an overriding concern for the growth and confidence of the coachee. When people don't see things that perhaps look obvious to us, we need to remember that they will have their own good reasons for not seeing. We can confront, but we should not force or bully. We should leave an escape route whereby people can continue not to see something if they need to.

Skilful confronting points out a puzzle. It does not provide the solution to the puzzle. That is for the person who is in the puzzle, and who has both more information and more investment, to do.

Chapter 7

Habits

Introduction

There isn't a neat distinction between 'skills', the subject of the last chapter, and 'habits', the subject of this one. But it seems to me that the skills described in Chapter 6 are essential. Without them a coach cannot be effective. The habits in this chapter are ways of behaving that are hugely helpful to the coaching effort, but not essential. Also, these habits are part of what makes for different coaching styles.

Some coaches have one or two of these habits very strongly, others have different ones. It will depend to some extent on the personality of the coach. There is choice and variety here. But I have seen every one of the habits described below put to very good effect by at least one skilful coach.

Like skills, habits can be practised and learned. I do think they need though, even more than the skills, to fit with the overall style, approach and preferences of an individual coach. If they seem 'stuck on' they will feel false, like a technique, to the coachee, and they will impair rather than assist her learning. And that is why I have called them 'habits', to communicate the need for them to come 'naturally'.

Self-awareness

It was particularly hard to decide whether 'self-awareness' should be considered a skill or a habit. Self-awareness to some degree is pretty much essential to coach effectively (and, it could be argued, to any kind of activity that depends on human interaction for its success), and I do believe it can be developed. (There is even a chapter on how coaches can help their coachees develop it later in the book, Chapter 14.)

But the habit of self-awareness, of remaining detached from your own actions and reactions to such a degree so that you are able to choose the ones that will be most helpful for your coachee, goes beyond straightforward self-awareness. Interestingly, I know people who have decided against a career in coaching because they don't want to become too conscious of their own actions and reactions. They worry that a habit of self-awareness could detract from their spontaneity and 'naturalness', and I believe they have a point.

But coaches who have the habit of self-awareness can offer their coachees a great deal. In Part Three, we shall talk about the coach using her own feelings and responses to provide vital information about her coachee. And in Part Four we shall see how a habit of self-awareness in the coach is the foundation of many practical tools and techniques, such as 'Telling the truth in the here and now' (in Chapter 14) and using 'Pitch, tone and pace of voice' to trigger a reflective state of mind (in Chapter 15).

Storytelling and metaphor making

Milton Erickson built his whole therapeutic practice on storytelling and metaphor making. People would come to him in distress and tell their stories, asking for help. Erickson did not tell them what to do or give them advice. He asked questions until he felt he understood that person and her context and what was important to her. Then he would tell a story.

Often there would be no links made in an explicit way between the story he told and the problem his patient had. But the story would have a strong impact on the patient because indeed Erickson had chosen it for its relevance to her. And the patient would solve her problem and be relieved of her distress because of what she had learned, often at an unconscious level, from Erickson's story.

If you are intrigued by Erickson's story-telling, you can read more in Sidney Rosen (1991).

A coach is not a therapist. He is unlikely to have the same level of training, supervision and skill as a therapist. He needs to work in more straightforward ways. He usually deals with people who are not in so much pain as most of a therapist's clients, and where he comes across someone who is he will probably need to refer them. Also, a coach of the kind we are focusing on in this book is first and foremost concerned with the individual at work.

Of course, that cannot be considered in isolation; think about the issue of work/life balance, for example. But coaching is more akin to assisted problem-solving, and therapy is more akin to healing. These are important distinctions.

Nonetheless, we have already learned about active listening from the psychotherapist Carl Rogers. And the work of Milton Erickson reminds us of the power of storytelling and metaphor making.

For millennia people have been telling each other stories that are coded messages about life and how to live. The Grimm Brothers' fairy tales, for example, enable children to explore and understand their strong sexual feelings, their ambivalence towards their parents, their jealousies and destructiveness, but in a way that is not too confronting, not too frightening.

Aesop's fables provide advice on how to live a good and successful life with stories about animals – much more memorable than a list of instructions, and much more likely to catch the imagination and stay in our minds, resurfacing at times when their message is most relevant. Which of us doesn't think of the hare and the tortoise when we're tempted to cut a corner to gain a short-term advantage, or when we seem to be losing out to a faster-moving rival and we need to reassure ourselves that winning now isn't everything?

When a coach has the habit of storytelling and metaphor making, that can help her coachees in ways that direct advice or statement of view cannot, and for the same reasons that stories have always been powerful. A story allows a potentially frightening topic to be talked about in an indirect way. Because it is a story, in other words a metaphor for some aspect of reality, but not a direct description of the reality, it allows the listener to understand the message at the level he can cope with.

If I were to say to a small child 'sometimes you want to kill your mother, and it's OK to feel that way', that would be a frightening description of reality she couldn't deal with. But if I tell her the story of Snow White, she can think about mothers, both good and bad, dying, and about the consequences; she can gain reassurance that strong feelings about parents are part of life and happen to other children too. The fact that an adult is telling the story reassures her that her destructive feelings are contained, they are known about and taken care of at some level.

So a story gives the listener the freedom to understand it and connect with it at the level most helpful, and bearable, to him. Storytelling is very different indeed from telling, and very appropriate for the purposes of coaching, where it is the coachee who needs to be in charge.

Second, as we have said, stories are more interesting to listen to and more memorable than advice. Coachees are likely already to have heard plenty of advice; a coach needs to be able to give them something different.

Finally, it is natural to tell stories. The habit of storytelling is building on a universal human tendency. It fits easily into a conversation.

Here is a simple example of storytelling in a coaching context. A partner in a firm of architects was working too hard. That was his view, and the view of his colleagues, and the view of his wife! He was working very long days without a break, had stopped going to the gym, and still felt all the time as if he was barely coping. He felt he was bad at delegating. But he didn't want to give up any aspect of his role.

His coach spent a couple of sessions exploring and understanding with him the nature of his situation and his feelings about it. She came to understand that he was someone who set himself high standards, and also that all aspects of his work mattered to him. He wouldn't be happy giving up either his client work or his management role.

> *Storytelling is very different indeed from telling, and very appropriate for the purposes of coaching, where it is the coachee who needs to be in charge.*

Then she thought of a story that seemed to her as if it might speak to him. It was a true story, as they often are.

A friend of hers ran his own business. He had been so busy that he was completely booked up for the next two months – not a single space in his diary. He was feeling very anxious about this, and also worried that he wasn't spending enough time with his children.

Then suddenly and tragically his father died. He had to go and support his mother, and in fact had to be away for three weeks. He made other arrangements for his work to be covered. Clients were understanding. When he returned to work, he had to take it easy at first because he was still distressed, but after a month or two everything was back to normal. His business had not been damaged in any way.

The coach told the architect this story. He listened intently. He asked questions about her friend to check he was really OK. And then he smiled and looked thoughtful. And he began to make changes. He booked sessions at the gym. He booked a holiday with his wife. He let it be known that he was taking every Friday afternoon off. What he had taken from the story was that often the only way for a perfectionist like himself to reduce the pressure is to be physically absent from the office for chunks of time, and that nothing collapses in your absence.

The architect had been told, and told himself, many times that he wasn't indispensable, and that he should take more time off. But when people told him that, he just thought of all the reasons why they were wrong. But the story interested him. It spoke to him in a different way. He took his own message from it. Also, he knew the story was true. It probably reminded him of other similar stories. It carried weight with him in a way a straightforward piece of advice would not.

Now, the habit of storytelling is only a good one if it's done in the right way. We have all known bad coaches who tell stories all the time – but they are stories that interest them, not stories carefully chosen because they will interest the coachee. (Some coaches tell too many stories about themselves, for example.) A good coaching story is told at the right time and in the right way. It should be easy for the coach to see whether the story is interesting her coachee or not, and if it doesn't, it can easily be cut short or discarded.

A story is a metaphor. But some coaches use metaphor more directly.

I remember a boss of mine who was trying to get me to deliver something I was bored with. She said: 'You had better be careful not to get a reputation as a black hole, Alison.' I was certainly motivated by that metaphor (some would even say manipulated by it): I was horrified at the picture of tasks disappearing into me and never getting done, and at the extreme damage to my reputation this might cause; the extremeness of the metaphor made me pay attention!

I'm not suggesting such a manipulative use of metaphor is a good idea for a coach. But when you want a coachee to pay particular attention to something, a well-chosen metaphor is often the way to do it. Metaphors that mean something particular to the coachee are the best.

For example, I know a coach who used metaphors from mountaineering to talk about team issues with an investment banker who was planning to climb in the Himalayas that summer. The use of such metaphors enriches the coachee's ways of thinking about old problems, and can lead him to new insights.

Laughing, and humour

A habit of seeing the funny side of things can be part of a coach's effectiveness. Now clearly, laughing at the coachee or in a way that jars, telling inappropriate jokes, and appearing not to take seriously things the coachee takes very seriously, are all bad habits. But we are assuming that the coach already has the appropriate beliefs and values, and the basic skills. So they will preclude a bad habit of humour.

The good habit of humour connects coach and coachee. Laughing with someone both establishes and confirms a level of mutual understanding. Hence the expression, 'to share a joke'. Laughter and humour raise energy levels. That is often necessary in a two-hour coaching session, which is a pretty intense and draining experience for many people. Laughter and humour engender optimism.

Remember that an optimistic view is important for coaching, where we are often trying to make progress on old and so far intractable issues. Laughter and humour are infectious, so the coachee ends up feeling more optimistic too. And laughter and humour encourage playfulness, which may lead to different ways of looking at things, new insights and change.

Some coaches are by nature pretty serious people. (So are some coachees.) They are not bad coaches. But coaches who have a habit of humour often bring something extra. They are likely to sense whether their coachee also has a habit of humour, and if they do, the coach will be able to use it very constructively.

I'm not sure that you can develop a habit of humour and laughing from scratch. But so long as you have a slight inclination that way (and most of us do), you can build on it. It is often associated with a tendency to see a situation in a surprising way.

I remember a coachee of mine who had a strong habit of seeing the ridiculous in just about everything. In fact, it caused him problems at work. It was as if he was always saying to himself 'what would a visitor from another planet make of all this?' And that made him laugh.

He was a delight to coach, because he used his tendency to see things in whacky ways to get ideas for dealing with things differently. He had some problems with a bully at work for a while. Together, we decided she had expanded like a huge balloon and what he needed to do was shrink her back to human size. We had a lot of fun working out how to do this and playing with the images.

Students of humour suggest that much humour stems from incongruity. When a toddler spills his drink, we don't laugh. It is only to be expected. When a policeman spills his drink, we do laugh. It is incongruous to see someone so neat in uniform, so much in control, suddenly lose control.

Sometimes humour alerts coachees to incongruity in what they are doing, and they decide to do something different.

I remember a management consultant who was hugely anxious about his relationship with his boss; she just didn't seem to value him. One day he arrived at the coaching session late, because he had had to deal with his 4-year-old's temper tantrum. He hadn't been giving her enough attention.

Suddenly, we both burst out laughing simultaneously. He said: 'I think I've been having a temper tantrum about my boss ... maybe it's time I grew up!' He saw the incongruity between his dependency on his boss and his mature professional status as a consultant.

Wondering

Coaches who are by nature very inquisitive, who spend a lot of their time wondering about things, engage their coachees in a journey of exploration that they may not have been on before. Like humour, wondering can be infectious, and it is a good thing for a coachee to catch. By wondering 'what would happen if ... ? or 'what he meant by that...?' the coachee may be led to find out more information or simply to see things in a different way. We have talked about how curiosity underpins the essential coaching skill of questioning. But a habit of wondering does even more.

A habit of wondering also communicates very clearly that the coach does not have, or feel he has, the answers. It allows him to raise possibilities speculatively, in a way that doesn't pressure the coachee into agreeing or disagreeing. It keeps thinking fluid, which helps prevent a too early and ill-considered rush to resolution.

Beware of coaches who start a sentence with 'I wonder if' when what they mean is 'I think that...' And beware of doing this as a coach. It is disingenuous, and can break the connection between coach and coachee.

Structuring and ordering

People sometimes come to coaching because they are confused, because they 'can't see the wood for the trees'. Often they are overwhelmed by the complexity of the situations they face and don't know where to start to sort things out. Given that many people choose coaching at major transition points in their lives, they are likely to have lost their way a little. They have important decisions to make, and a mass of information they need to attend to.

I remember a coachee who said: 'When I was just a client lawyer, everything seemed very simple. I had my systems for keeping things under control. Now I have management responsibilities I just seem to hurtle from one meeting to the next.'

At such times of temporary bewilderment, a coach with a habit of structuring and ordering can be a godsend. Such coaches take all the data they are learning from their coachee, and say things like, 'It looks as if the two most urgent things are … would that be right?' Or 'how about we focus on this thing today, and leave the other things till next week?' Such coaches are also likely to be orderly in their approach to the coaching relationship itself, encouraging a regularity and predictability in the pattern of meetings, having particular ways of opening and closing sessions.

One coach I know starts every session with the simple question 'What's up?' It's a signal to his coachees that they have now entered a time that is for them alone and in which they can talk about whatever's on their mind. The predictable opening is calming and reassuring for busy people who normally never know what's going to hit them next.

Coaches with a habit of structuring and ordering are likely to encourage their coachees to make specific plans, and to check on their progress. They will suggest ways for the coachee to measure progress, and even provide forms and templates to help them.

But the most valuable thing they do for coachees is make some orderly sense of what the coachee is saying, thinking and feeling. A coachee often talks non-stop in the early sessions of coaching, pouring out all her thoughts on what's happened, what's going on, and what she hopes for. A coach with the habit of structuring and ordering, with a tidy mind, if you like, can lend his tidy mind to the coachee.

He can summarise and suggest priorities, in a way that increases the coachee's sense of being in control of her life. He will only be telling her things she has already told him. But he will be telling her those things in an order and with a pattern she had not seen them in before. If he has listened to her carefully, that order and that pattern will make sense to her.

Like all the habits, this one can be taken to extremes. I know coaches who have rigid methodologies and impose these on all coachees. That means they will not be effective for many. A habit of ordering and structuring is good when it is directed to helping others. When it is directed towards feeling safe and secure yourself, it limits your ability to help others.

I think a habit of structuring and ordering can definitely be developed. In Part Four we introduce some ordering and structuring frameworks and tools any coach can use well.

Consequences

I wasn't sure what to call this habit. But it is very useful indeed. In some ways it is a mix of habits: a habit of logical thinking combined with an ability to maintain detachment laced with a large dose of insight and compassion. I think it is the habit that underpins what Mike Brearley sums up as the two essential characteristics of a coach: 'empathy and robustness'. What all that results in is a coach who helps a coachee understand the consequences of the choices she has made and might make. So the coachee is better informed when she makes her next set of choices.

But actually the real benefit of 'consequences' is something rather different, and quite subtle. We all go through phases when we feel we're the victims. We feel powerless, and at the mercy of how others choose to behave. Now since coaching is about empowering the coachee, it is important that it should encourage the opposite of this 'victim' mentality. The habit of consequences does just that. It doesn't recommend courses of action. It prompts the coachee to explore what the consequences of the different possible courses might be. It communicates the philosophy that you always have choice, that certain outcomes will follow certain choices, that you are choosing those outcomes when you make those choices, and that generally, no choice will guarantee either disaster or triumph. It will simply lead to the next set of choices.

Coaches who have the habit of consequences ask questions such as 'how will so-and-so react?', 'how will that affect you?', 'can you see any risks?' and so on. They are encouraging their coachees to imagine all the paths they might take, and what it will actually mean to travel each path. In fact, they are coaching their coachees in the habit of consequences. And that is a very useful habit to have, not just for coaches. How often have you said 'If I knew then what I know now...'? Consequences means you can.

> *Since coaching is about empowering the coachee, it is important that it should encourage the opposite of this 'victim' mentality. The habit of consequences does just that.*

You may be wondering where the 'insight' and 'compassion' I mentioned as being part of this habit of consequences comes in. Surely I have just been describing logical thinking applied precisely to an individual's issues?

Not at all. It is the insight and the compassion that make the habit of consequences so powerful. The insight guides the coach to explore the consequences she understands will be most important to the coachee. There isn't time to explore them all. But some will really affect the coachee. Those are the ones it is most important to identify.

I remember coaching someone who had to decide whether to give a big presentation. She was frightened of doing it but thought she ought to. This was a classic case for 'playing consequences'. Among other things, I asked her how she would feel the day after the presentation if she didn't do it. I knew her to be a person who valued courage and bravery. I knew it was important for her to consider the consequences in terms of how she would feel about her own courage and bravery. (Incidentally, she decided she would feel fine the next day. She would look for an opportunity to give a presentation about a subject she was more confident in.)

The compassion is about the coach understanding that people don't always feel good about the choices they make. They can see that in the universe of possible consequences they have made the best choice they can. But maybe they still feel sad or disappointed. The coach has helped them choose intelligently. But she could not change the nature of the choices they had to make; life was still 'a bitch' at that point in time. If she appreciates that, she will help the coachee explore consequences with much more sensitivity and skill than if she regards it as an exercise in logic.

The detachment is of course, as ever, about the coach not having a view on which choice is best. How could she presume to know?

Chapter 8

Actions

Introduction

Often it is little things that make the difference in a relationship. So we end this part of the book, on the coach, with a look at some of the little things that coaches do that make or mar their relationship with their coachees.

I have organised these little things, specific actions, using David Maister's formula for how trust is built in a professional relationship. It is relevant here because if we had to characterise the nature of a good coaching relationship in one word we should probably choose 'trust'.

So I shall categorise the actions according to whether they affect the 'credibility', the 'reliability', the 'intimacy', or the 'perceived self-orientation' of the coach. These four dimensions are the key components of trust, according to Maister's formula (see *The Trusted Advisor* by Maister et al. 2002 for more details).

One final point needs to be made. In many ways actions are nothing more than, and nothing less than, symptoms of the deeper truths about the values, beliefs and motives of the coach. For example, a coach who respects others and their ways of seeing the world is unlikely to take the action of interrupting her coachee on a regular basis. Constant interruption is a symptom of disrespect.

As symptoms, such actions help us identify who is appropriately equipped to be a coach. But as symptoms they are not things that in themselves will guarantee a coach builds trust readily. A coach who holds back from interrupting may be welcome to the coachee, but such restraint will hardly alone establish the coach's positive intent. Unless specific actions stem from strong feelings the coach has about what is important, their impact is likely to be fleeting and superficial.

Actions that build or damage the coach's 'credibility'

Credibility is about people believing we can do what we say we can. When a coach identifies resources that may help the coachee (books, courses, other people), this builds it. When a coach displays some relevant knowledge, shows she has relevant tools and techniques at her disposal, this builds it. When a coach addresses the issue of her fee straightforwardly and confidently, this builds it too. And it is good for a coach's credibility when she can give examples of other times she has helped people (without boasting or breaking confidences).

In many ways, the thing that builds a coach's credibility best is an action someone else takes: it is when someone whom the coachee respects says 'she coached me and it was really helpful'. So the coach is on the best footing so far as her credibility is concerned when someone has personally recommended her.

Hesitancy about matters that concern her own professional standards and ways of working undermines credibility.

I know an excellent coach, one of the most skilful and knowledgeable in the business and someone to whom I sometimes go for coaching. He has undermined his credibility on more than one occasion because he has a hesitant manner and sometimes does not speak clearly, concisely, and authoritatively about how coaching should proceed.

Getting something wrong and blustering rather than cheerfully admitting it undermines credibility badly. For example, coaches are human and may misremember something a coachee has told them. Or they may get confused about the structure of the organisation the coachee works in. Such errors are only problems if we react defensively. If we do, the coachee wonders 'what else does he have to hide?'

Actions that build 'reliability'

The coachee wants to know not only whether we can do what we say we can, but whether we will do what we promise. That is reliability. To build it, we should look for opportunity to demonstrate it in small things.

We should promise to phone and do so. We should undertake to find something out by the next session and make sure we do. We should follow up on things that were talked about in previous sessions. We should manage the time in our coaching sessions well, so that we do what we said we would. When we return phone calls quickly, we build reliability.

Interestingly, there is another side to reliability. People feel a coach is reliable when he shows by his actions that he knows what they like, what they feel comfortable with.

I know a coach whose reliability plummeted because he suggested meeting his coachee in her home. She wondered how he could not have sensed that she would find that inappropriate – she is a very private person. My reliability increased when I offered to summarise a coachee's development plan for him. That is exactly what he had been hoping for.

Reliability is built when a coachee's expectations, both explicitly agreed and implicitly felt, are met.

Lateness damages reliability. So does cancelling sessions at short notice, changing times and venues, and surprising your coachee with an unexpected agenda.

'Intimacy'

The kind of 'intimacy' we are talking about here has to do with the coachee feeling comfortable with the coach. If she feels she knows him well enough to predict how he will behave in the different situations she may work with him in, she will feel comfortable.

Typically, intimacy – and comfortableness – rise the better we know someone. So whenever the coach discloses something about how he is feeling, intimacy rises. That is not to say the coach should be talking about his feelings all the time, or at the expense of what the coachee needs to talk about. He should talk about his feelings in relation to the work he and the coachee are doing. When he reveals his personal response, he builds intimacy.

For example, he may feel unsure of what to do next, excited about a particular way of thinking, disappointed that he hasn't been able to help the coachee make more progress. Far from being a distant and all-wise counsellor, the coach should be honestly human. The more transparent his values, beliefs and motives are, the more trustworthy he will be. When he acknowledges his own shortcomings as a coach it may feel risky to him, but it will build intimacy.

An air of imperturbability reduces intimacy. So do formulae for working. And so does being right all the time (how human is that?).

'Perceived self-orientation'

This gets to the heart of things. It is about whether the coachee feels that the coach really cares. What a coach needs to establish is a *lack* of self-orientation in the coachee's eyes. And she will be on the look-out for signs that he cares about her, and signs that he cares more about himself.

If a coachee needs to cancel a session at short notice because she is under pressure, being happy to let her do so and flexible about rear-ranging shows you care. (And the converse is true: rigid insistence on contractual agreements can undermine a coaching relationship.) Being available when it isn't convenient for you but it is important to the coachee also helps.

Looking after the coachee's physical needs – the temperature of the room, the comfort of the chairs, the availability of water or coffee – is a sign the coach cares, and will be taken as such. Wanting to know what happens and asking the coachee to stay in touch, even when the coaching has formally finished, is important. Sending Christmas cards, remembering the coachee's birthday, phoning the coachee at important times for her; all this demonstrates that it is 'not just' a work contract. It is a human relationship in which the coach cares about the coachee's success.

Sometimes coaches fight shy of these actions, worrying that they might become 'personally involved'. But a coach needs to be personally involved to establish trust. He is not personally involved for his own needs, but personally involved for his coachee's. That is the difference between inappropriate and appropriate personal involvement.

A final point here is important. The coach should show pleasure when things go well for the coachee no matter who is responsible. If it is all her own work, that is best of all. If someone else has helped her, great. If a coach finds himself behaving as if he needs to be the one who helps, he is showing that he cares more about himself than her. It will damage trust.

PART THREE

THE COACHING RELATIONSHIP

Introduction

Throughout Parts One and Two of this book, we have referred to coaching as a relationship. But we have focused on the individuals in that relationship: first, the coachee; and then the coach. What happens between them is just as important.

Typically a person who is looking for a coach will spend some time with a potential coach before committing to having coaching with that individual. Or they will have had the chance to get to know the potential coach in another context first. People will say this testing-out is important because the success of coaching depends in large part on 'the chemistry' between coach and coachee.

I would say that, like all relationships, coaching has a set of dynamics – constantly changing rules determining how the individuals behave towards each other – and these dynamics need to be understood and managed. The 'chemistry' is to do with the extent they are successfully understood and managed – primarily by the coach. If the coachee becomes aware of them that suggests the coach is not doing his job well. At that point, the relationship between coach and coachee has come into the foreground, and will distract from the coach's relationship with her own objectives. But that happens from time to time, and all will not be lost, so long as coach and coachee can appreciate what's going on and get things back on the right track. This part of the book aims to help them do just that.

Chapter 9

The key dynamics

Introduction

In this chapter we shall use the psychologist Schutz's formulation of what goes on when two or more people try to form and maintain a relationship. His ideas are clear and extensively researched (see, for example, his book *The Human Element*, 1994). Also, they, or ideas obviously similar to them, crop up all the time in descriptions of how teams form and fail, of why crowds behave as they do, and of many other domains of social interaction. We can have confidence that they capture the key dynamics of relationship.

Needs to give, and needs to get

The first thing to understand is that we all have needs in relation to other people, and there is great variety in what those needs are. One person may need to feel liked by most people they meet, while another needs to be liked by a select few (she is indifferent to or even contemptuous of the multitude). One person needs the people around her to give her clarity about what they expect from her, while another needs people to 'stay off her case'.

When one person meets another and they naturally give each other what they need, the 'chemistry' works. When one person cannot give the other what she needs, it will still be possible for them to relate to each other, but there will always be moments of jarring, disappointment and regretted compromise. You will readily see that it is rare for one person to meet another's needs completely, and rare for there to be no satisfaction whatsoever. For most of our relationships, most of the time, it is a question of degree.

The second thing to understand is that we don't just need things from other people, we need to give things to them as well. Will Schutz called these two kinds of need 'wanted' (we want to receive) and 'expressed' (we want to give out). To feel fully ourselves and valued as

70

such, we are dependent both on others' behaving in certain ways to us and on their accepting certain behaviours from us. So I may need others to give me a lot of feedback. But I may also need to give them a lot. Or a little. (We don't always want the same from others as we want to give out to them.)

Also, what we need from others depends on what we already have, on what stage a relationship is at, on what is going on in that relationship. I may need a lot of feedback when I have just had a row with someone, but only a little when we are working harmoniously together, for example. So that is why we talk about the 'dynamics': things are moving and changing all the time.

Coaches will be most effective when they can follow and respond to the interpersonal needs their coachee has of them. This is quite distinct from their needs in relation to 'the coaching work' that we shall discuss later. It is to do with getting the basic chemistry right, which then enables effective work. For example, suppose my coachee needs me to show warmth to her. If I don't, she will be preoccupied and disappointed (although she may not know why) and she won't be able to work so well. If I do meet her needs for warmth, she will forget about them and turn her attention to the work.

Let us look now at the three types of social need, which, if left unattended to, will damage the coaching relationship and get in the way of good work.

Needs related to belonging

As social animals, we know that our success and even our survival depend on having a place in a society. We are sensitive to whether we fit in, or misfit. We are constantly, and largely unconsciously, checking whether we are like those we are with, and whether they are like us.

It is not just that we need to belong full stop. We need to belong to groups that confirm how we want to see ourselves and enhance our feelings of significance. Imagine a teenager walking into a classroom at a college for a course in Spanish and discovering all the other students were over 40. Most teenagers would walk straight out again! They need to belong to groups that confirm their youth and rebelliousness.

In the coaching relationship, the coachee's needs for belonging will be to do with whether she feels the coach is sufficiently 'like' her (and like how she needs to see herself) and whether she feels that being coached by this particular individual 'fits' with what 'people like her' would do. That is one reason why personal recommendation is such a good way (although not without its drawbacks) for people to find coaches.

A coachee recently came to me who had just been made redundant. His boss, who despite the redundancy, this coachee liked and respected, had had a few coaching sessions with me, and had recommended me to his departing colleague. The fact that I had been his boss's coach was very important to this man, whose needs to belong were high at this time.

By recommending his own coach, his boss was sending a message that this man was still included in his boss's social system. This beginning guaranteed that my coachee would not be troubled by his needs for belonging; they had already been taken care of.

By the same token, it is unlikely a coachee will 'gel' with a coach who has been recommended to him by someone he doesn't like. He won't want to be 'the kind of person' who is coached by them!

As we have already said, different people have different levels of need for inclusion.

I was introduced to a senior manager in the City whose need to belong was practically non-existent. In fact, it was more of a need 'not to belong'! He rejected a number of coaches, probably because they were too much from his world, they had *too* much in common with him. He eventually chose as a coach someone with a psychotherapy background who had never had a client in the City before.

> *We need to belong to groups that confirm how we want to see ourselves and enhance our feelings of significance.*

Most people do have inclusion needs, though. They are likely to be particularly significant in the early stages of a coaching relationship because that relationship tends to be a close rather than a distant one. So it carries more implications for the coachee's view of himself and of where he fits. (To understand this point, imagine how much less you would care about the social background of your milkman than that of your life partner.)

A coach can put inclusion needs to rest in part by showing that he understands the 'society' the coachee belongs to (is familiar with the organisation, has relationships with other people the coachee knows, abides by the social 'norms' the coachee is used to – things like dress, manner of greeting, and so on). But there is more to it than this.

The coachee is likely to be asking himself before committing to a coach 'Am I the kind of person who would have coaching with this coach? Do I want to be? What does it say about me if I do?' There are really only two things the coach can do about this. First, and most important, she needs to have dealt with her own needs to belong and to feel significant. She needs to feel comfortable with her place in society.

(Sometimes I wonder about the wisdom of using retired people as coaches for folk who are still working in the organisation. It may make the coachee nervous that perhaps he isn't totally part of the organisation any more, just as his coach isn't. And when retired people haven't come to terms with their retirement – and it takes a while – their own discomfort with their place in society will make it more difficult for them to meet their coachee's needs to belong.)

The second thing the coach can do is to be very open and clear about where she does actually fit. If that leaves the coachee uncomfortable, with anxieties about being coached by 'a person like this,' then it's better for another coach to be found. It will be put down to 'chemistry'.

For example, I am always very open about being a psychologist. I take care to explain what it means, but I don't hide it: it is a part of my identity I am very comfortable with. Some people don't want to be coached by a psychologist. They worry that it puts them in the same group as 'mentally ill' people or 'stressed people'. They have needs to belong to another group, and they will get on better with a business coach, or a sportsperson, for example.

In fact, one of the commonest reasons for people rejecting coaching altogether is because they have come to the view 'People like me don't need a coach.' And that is sometimes a very good reason. If every time such a coachee has a session she is troubled by what having coaching says about her, it is unlikely she will get much from those sessions.

The issue of inclusion, or need to belong, is usually resolved in the early stages of the coaching relationship and is then unlikely to resurface. Either the coach meets the coachee's needs on this dimension satisfactorily, or she doesn't and the relationship ends. The dynamic aspect of which the coach needs to be aware is that the coachee's needs for inclusion at the point in time when he meets her will be heavily influenced by what is going on in her other relationships at that time.

We saw above an example where the coachee had just been made redundant, and the impact that had. Other significant events influencing how much and by whom a coachee needs to be included are a change of employer, role and/or team, departure of a boss or important colleague, change of company management, and so on: in short, anything that rocks the coachee's sense of having a secure place in a social group that fits her aspirations.

Needs related to controlling

Anyone who has experienced the 'storming' stage of team development will easily understand the importance and force of our needs related to controlling, and being controlled by, others. Once people have got to know each other a little, the power struggle begins, the fight to determine everyone's place in the pecking order. These control needs are particularly intense in groups, which remind people of their families complete with sibling rivalry, and which also elicit unconscious ancient memories of tribal life.

Fortunately, coaching is generally a one-to-one relationship, and the needs related to controlling and being controlled by others are less intense. But just as they also surface between individuals in a marriage, even though there are only two of them, so they do make an appearance in the coaching relationship.

It is important to remember that needs to have control, or for someone else to take control, are at their root to do with our need to feel competent, able to deal with whatever life requires us to. If we feel overwhelmed by someone else's will and directions, then we begin to feel as if we do not have charge of our own lives. That is frightening; our survival could be at risk. Similarly, if we are overwhelmed by complexity and ambiguity, we experience the same kind of fear. When so-called 'power struggles' begin, the answer will lie not in a fight but in restoring the feelings of competence of both parties.

This is best done through a flexible and responsive 'power-sharing' relationship between coach and coachee. Whether the coachee begins in a state of submissiveness, apparently needing the coach to take charge, or storms in with a list of demands as if the coach were a member of staff, apparently needing to be in total control, or anywhere in between, the coach needs to establish the principle and practice of negotiation early on.

There is good opportunity to do so: first the agenda for the first meeting needs to be agreed, and both parties' wants and views are relevant; the coach needs to learn some background from the coachee, and vice versa; they need to work together to agree scheduling of sessions, purpose of the coaching and so on. By the end of the session, the control dynamic should have settled into a relaxed adult-to-adult exchange. The competence of both coach and coachee will have been affirmed.

If the coachee is inclined to be rather passive, she may need the coach to take control for a while to meet her needs for control from another; with judicious questioning he should then be able to pass control to her, but in a structured way that she finds reassuring. As her needs for him to take control are met, their intensity subsides. If the coach mistakenly tries to manage the dynamic by refusing to take control, maybe by saying for example 'what we do is completely up to you; it's your session' then her needs will intensify and the relationship is likely to break down.

Similarly, if the coachee needs to exert a lot of control, laying down chapter and verse and dominating the interaction (which of course may often be done just as much through nonverbal communication as through words), then the coach is best listening carefully and letting her have her say, acknowledging wherever this can be done honestly the truth and appropriateness of

> It is important to remember that needs to have control, or for someone else to take control, are at their root to do with our need to feel competent, able to deal with whatever life requires us to.

what she is saying; then her needs to be in charge will lessen, and the coach can put some of his own thoughts and views across. Again, if the coach tries to fight for control, the coachee is likely to get increasingly controlling and the relationship to break down.

I have described managing the control dynamic at the start of the relationship. But control needs fluctuate throughout a relationship. When something happens that causes a coachee anxiety about her or her coach's competence, she will typically respond with either an increase in submissive behaviour or an increase in controlling behaviour (which she chooses will depend on her preferred style; a coach will soon recognise what her typical style is). Each time this happens, the coach needs to move back towards power-sharing by first of all meeting the coachee's needs, and then, when the anxiety has subsided, starting to negotiate in the way I have described.

Needs related to closeness

We learn about closeness at our mother's (and father's) knee. We may be brought up with a lot of demonstrated affection and warmth, or we may be brought up in a more emotionally distant way where each member of the family is encouraged to be emotionally self-sufficient (although nonetheless loved and looked after), or we may be brought up somewhere in between these two extremes.

However it happens, the style of our upbringing in relation to closeness and distance has a profound impact on our needs as adults for warmth, openness and affection. And these needs run deep, tend to remain much the same throughout our lives, and determine the nature of all our important personal relationships.

These are the last needs we shall look at in this chapter. They are relevant to most of our work relationships, and they are certainly relevant to the coaching relationship. If a coach is a very 'close and personal' individual, this will work well for someone with high needs for closeness. Such a coachee will be reassured that the relationship is sound, and will move on to do the work. But if a coach like this meets a potential coachee who prefers distance, her coachee is likely to experience her as intrusive, inappropriate and over-emotional. The mismatch will disrupt the coaching relationship and undermine the work.

Just as serious a mismatch can happen when a coach who maintains a fair degree of interpersonal distance meets a coachee who needs a lot of closeness.

Too great a mismatch on such a fundamental dimension of human need suggests that potential coach and coachee should just 'call it a day'. But most of the time there are things the coach can do to ensure a better dynamic in respect of this need.

First, the coach needs to know himself. He needs to ask himself (and others whom he trusts) questions like: Do I like to get close to people? Do I like them to get close to me? Do I know a lot about my family, friends and close colleagues – in terms of their hopes and fears, their 'hot buttons', their dreams and nightmares? Do I know what they think about me? Do they know what I think about them? The more he gets the answer 'yes' to questions like this, the more of a 'close and personal' coach he is likely to be. Lots of 'no' answers suggest a more formal approach.

Then the coach needs to ask himself: are my needs being met in my life generally? If they are, he will be more able to set them to one side in the coaching relationship and respond to the coachee.

As a consequence of understanding himself, the coach will be on the look-out for people who need something different from what he would naturally give. When he comes across such a person, he needs to control his own needs and respond to hers.

If she needs a bit more distance, he should be sparing with questions she would find 'personal', and he should focus on the facts and on a businesslike, professional approach. He should focus on the coaching assignment and not on the relationship between him and her. He should let her take the lead in moving on to personal perspectives and issues.

If, on the other hand, she needs more warmth from him, he should spend more time getting to know her, and be more open about his own experiences and feelings. She may welcome the opportunity to get to know him better, over lunch or a coffee.

As with many aspects of human interaction, it is rigidity that makes things difficult. For example, a coach with an extreme and unmet need for closeness is unlikely to be flexible enough to meet the needs of a more 'distant' coachee. Coaches who are successful with lots of different people tend to be more adaptable in their own needs on this dimension, able to enjoy both close and more distant relationships, not having extreme and unmet needs of their own that clamour to be satisfied.

Recognising mismatches early

When things go awry in the dynamics of a relationship, often it is true that 'a stitch in time saves nine'. In fact, if the coach can recognise early that a mismatch is occurring between his behaviour and his coachee's needs, it may allow him to put things right that could otherwise spiral out of control. The coach has in fact the best 'early warning system' of all readily at his disposal. It is his own feelings.

You may remember in Chapter 4 where we said all human beings are good at sensing the underlying feelings and intentions of those we come into contact with. We pick up tiny clues, often at an unconscious level. We notice tiny changes in skin colour, voice tone, expression, position and so on (unconsciously); we process what that means (unconsciously); and then we feel something ourselves. It is at that point of feeling that what has been unconscious becomes conscious. So our feelings are our early warning system; they are the first sign we are aware of that something is going on.

It is vital for a coach to spend a little time immediately after every coaching session just reflecting on how he felt during the session, and how he feels now. It is not narcissistic. It is in order to check whether he is meeting his coachee's needs.

- Does he feel as if he might not be the right coach for this person after all? Then maybe her needs for belonging have come to the surface and not been met.
- Does he feel incompetent, angry or frustrated? Then maybe the coachee's control needs have not been met.
- Does he feel that he and his coachee aren't communicating very well? Then perhaps the distance between them isn't right for her.

Any anxiety at all needs to be attended to. If the coach examines his own anxiety in relation to the dimensions of interpersonal need of the coachee, and tries to work out where it is coming from, he will be well placed to put something right before the coachee has even consciously noticed what was wrong.

Of course, he may choose to talk about his anxiety explicitly with the coachee. But the vast majority of mismatches between coach behaviour and coachee need are best dealt with by small 'course corrections' by the coach, not by big and potentially disruptive 'pow-wows' between coach and coachee.

> *It is vital for a coach to spend a little time immediately after every coaching session just reflecting on how he felt during the session, and how he feels now.*

Chapter 10

The roles

Introduction

'Coach' is not a single role. That is one of the things people find confusing about coaching. They listen to one person talk about her coach and how he supported her through a very stressful few months; then they hear someone else describe how his coach helped him put together a strategic plan for his part of the business; and then they come across yet somebody else whose coach 'keeps her sane' as a working mother and has done so for over five years.

It is hard for people to see how all these very different things can go under the same label of 'coaching'. But when you remember, as we said in the Preface, that coaching is the activity whereby one person helps another to articulate and achieve their goals, through conversation, then it becomes clear that the 'help' might take many forms and the 'goals' be various and diverse. So a coach might need to fulfil many roles.

In this chapter we look at a range of typical roles a coach will play in order to achieve the overall purpose of coaching. Sometimes the coachee always wants the same role from her coach, but more typically a coach will move from one role to another over different sessions, and even within a session. Each role presents its own opportunities and risks, and we shall look at these.

In Part Four, we look at the different kinds of work coach and coachee do together. And of course, there is a strong link between the work you are doing and the role you are taking. But role addresses the question directly: 'What does my coach think she is? And what do I think she is?' The way that question is answered has profound effects on expectations and effectiveness. So it is worth exploring the issue of role, as well as the issue of work.

Coach as sounding board

Often what people need when they are trying to bring about some change is someone to listen and respond as they talk through different ideas and possible courses of action. They need to explore what their ideas really mean, in detail and in practice, through both hearing themselves talk about them and through hearing another person's response to them. They need a 'sounding board'.

A coach is well qualified to take this role because she is likely to be a good listener. She is likely also to be a good questioner, so she will ask the coachee questions that lead him to a much broader and deeper understanding of what he is proposing. She is unlikely to have any vested interests of her own in the topics under discussion (and if she does, she will have set them to one side in order to coach effectively). If she has worked as a coach to the individual for some time, she will know enough about him and his context to respond in an intelligent and relevant way.

All coaching will involve the coach as sounding board to some degree. Sometimes that is 'all' the coach does. Apart from the primary function of this role that we have just described, it is a great opportunity for the coach to learn more about the coachee, her way of thinking, and how she sees her world.

The risk is that the coach doesn't stick to 'sounding board' and strays into 'critic'. There is a fine but important distinction. A sounding board responds; a critic judges. A sounding board is your equal; a critic takes a superior position. A sounding board adds his thoughts to yours; a critic replaces your thoughts with his.

Here is an example of a coach doing a good job as a sounding board.

A colleague of mine was coaching a businessman who had been offered another job. He described the new opportunity, and the consequences, both good and bad, of taking it. My colleague asked him lots of questions, and as a result he explored more consequences than he would otherwise have done. He considered the consequences for his

All coaching will involve the coach as sounding board to some degree. Sometimes that is 'all' the coach does.

self-esteem of moving and not moving, and the consequences for his family relationships, for example. My colleague also commented on the way he was talking about his current company and way he was talking about the new one; she noticed some differences that seemed to her important.

The businessman floated various possibilities for himself, ranging from resigning immediately to pushing for promotion in his current company, and so on. He mused on the advantages and disadvantages of all of them. Towards the end of his decision-making, he said to my colleague: 'What would you do, if you were me?' She told him. He was interested; it led to some more discussion; in the end he decided not to leave.

Being a sounding board sounds deceptively easy. It isn't. To be fully immersed in another person's situation and possibilities, and not to start thinking you know what they should do, requires tough discipline. It requires all the resources of respect (see Chapter 4) we can muster.

Coach as conscience

I have a coachee who knows that when the pressure is on, he can get very demanding and directive with his staff. He also knows that when he thinks about how he is treating people he treats them well. He has appointed me his 'conscience'.

He wants to meet with me fairly infrequently, and for me to ask him about how his management of people has been going since I last saw him, and about what challenges in that area are coming up for him. He knows that just having those meetings with me will help him remember the people, and that being asked to talk about them every so often will help him establish a habit of care that will mitigate his forceful style even when the pressure is on.

Coaches are also often asked by their coachees to 'police' their work/life balance. Again, being asked every so often about your working hours, about whether you feel you are in balance, about whether your commitments to yourself and your family and your friends are being met as well as your commitments to your work, helps you to pay attention to the balance and take steps to improve it. Anything that has attention paid to it, particularly by someone afforded the status of coach, will move up the priority list.

Whenever a coachee asks a coach to remind him, make sure he doesn't forget, stop him doing something, check whether he has done something, and so on, the coach is being asked to be a 'conscience'. It is a limited role, but can be useful as part of what a coach does.

The important thing is not to become responsible for the behaviour of the coachee. That can't be helpful; for one thing, it puts the coach in an inappropriate power relationship, where she is in a way 'managing' the coachee in respect of a particular issue; for another thing, it makes it less likely the coachee will do anything himself – he has delegated responsibility to his coach!

I became concerned when a chief executive I worked with asked me to point out to him, and 'give him a hard time', whenever I saw him reacting in an inappropriately angry way with a particular member of his management team. I did comply for a couple of weeks, but his behaviour towards this individual got worse, not better. I was not being helpful as a 'conscience' here.

Coach as challenger

This role has similarities to 'coach as conscience' but it is more forceful. What many people lack – and, sadly, senior people lack this most of all – is honest challenge of their views and actions. They may get challenge, but often it is contaminated by the agenda of the person doing the challenging.

I coached an HR manager once who was being challenged on a regular basis by his boss to take more of a strategic view and seize opportunities to transform the way his team serviced the organisation. This HR manager knew that it would serve his boss's political agenda very well if he did that, and he wasn't sure whether it was the right thing for his team.

Now it was certainly true, and the HR manager would acknowledge this, that he did have a tendency to get embroiled in the operational agenda and ignore the strategic. But he couldn't disentangle in his boss's challenge what was true and what was simply expedient for his boss. Also, he was angry with his boss for, as he saw it, blaming him for being too operational when that boss was the one overloading him with operational responsibilities! With so much complexity and resentment around, it was extremely unlikely that the boss's challenge would do that HR manager any good.

Honest challenge is also hard for senior people to come by because people are often frightened of the consequences.

So a coach is often uniquely positioned to fulfil this important role. I remember a coachee who sought me out at a time when his career had hit a very rough patch. One of the things he said to me in our first meeting was 'I wanted you as my coach because I knew you wouldn't be easy on me.' I knew then that one of the roles he wanted me to take was that of challenging his thinking.

When a coach takes up the role of challenger, she needs to be careful that her coachee doesn't feel she has moved from being on 'his side' to being against him.

In the example I have just given, one of the things the coachee said was that he believed his position in the organisation to be secure because he was always being asked to do work by his internal clients. After some probing, we realised that these clients were not actually paying for his services; his time was allocated to a completely separate budget, about which his 'clients' neither knew nor cared.

In challenging him to explore the implications of this, I had to be very careful not to appear to be saying 'Actually you aren't really valued at all' (of course not a view I held, but one that my coachee, at this time of vulnerability, might easily have heard). In Part Four we shall look at how to confront skilfully, and that is very relevant here.

The role of challenger is invaluable when there is something highly relevant to progress on the coachee's goals that they either haven't thought of or are avoiding thinking about. But too much challenging implies the coachee cannot work things out for herself. That is undermining the basic purpose and philosophy of coaching.

Adrian Moorhouse experienced many different styles of coaching as he developed as a swimmer, and he draws a fundamental distinction between 'transactional' and 'transformational' coaching.

> *When a coach takes up the role of challenger, she needs to be careful that her coachee doesn't feel she has moved from being on 'his side' to being against him.*

- 'Transactional' is directive and 'challenging', in the sense we are using the word here. It challenges the coachee directly with an instruction to do something new or different. An example from Adrian's world would be 'You're too low in the water – get higher.'
- 'Transformational' is developing the coachee's ability to learn and develop himself. An example would be 'What do you notice about your height in the water?'

Both kinds of coaching are effective, used at the right time. But Adrian comments that he saw too many swimmers 'paralysed on the starting block' because they had had too much transactional coaching, too little transformational. They were left disabled by a lack of confidence in their own ability to decide how to swim their best. He decided to seek out coaching that enabled, rather than disabled, him.

Nonetheless, he considers his first and most important coach to have been both an enabler and a disabler, and that both strands of coaching played their part. He had some really combative moments with Adrian, which had a profound impact.

One such was when Adrian had come late to training three times in a row (he was going through a difficult time outside of the pool) and his coach simply shouted at him: 'I don't care about your problems with your girlfriend, just get in the pool and swim!' Adrian comments: 'I was upset, but I knew where he stood.' He wasn't late again, and also he began to make efforts to focus more on his swimming despite what was going on elsewhere. The direct challenge jolted him into some more productive behaviour.

Coming from the very different worlds of cricket and psychoanalysis, Mike Brearley too emphasises the importance of balancing the roles of 'facilitator' and 'confronter'. (You may remember we talked about the skill of confronting in Chapter 6.) Mike describes it in this way.

> 'Speaking generally, we might divide the task of coaching into two. One part involves finding the strengths of the individual or team, and working to create an environment in which these can flourish. The other part of the task is spotting those areas that need changing, and finding ways of confronting the team or the individual with these shortcomings.'

In Chapter 1, we had an example of Mike 'facilitating' excellent performance from Ian Botham in the 1981 Headingley test. He also confronted, in the same test, and to equally good effect. He describes one such effective 'confronting' intervention with Botham like this.

> 'Ian's bowling was not "free"; from close quarters on the field, I was alarmed to see that over the past year he had adopted a more delicate and less direct approach to the stumps, taking an exaggerated step in towards them in his delivery stride. He was trying to force his body round so as to make the ball swing. But the whole thing was done at half-pace; he left himself with no margin for error in length or direction, and the batsman had plenty of time to follow the ball's swing. I refused to go along with that stilted tide. I nick-named him "Sidestep Queen", and took him off after only three overs.

> 'At this point, the conversation went something like this. "How can I bowl in three-over spells?" "And how can I keep you on if you bowl medium-paced half-volleys?" In his next spell, he was quicker, more direct, more hostile.'

Deciding how often, and when, to take the role of challenger is one of the key things a coach must pay attention to. She needs to observe carefully the effect her challenging has. Does it liberate the coachee from some behaviour he had got stuck in? Or does it mire him in uncertainty and passivity?

Coach as teacher

Sometimes the coach knows how to do something the coachee does not. Sometimes the coach has some experience or knows something or someone that the coachee could benefit from knowing too. Then the coach may take the role of teacher, and pass the knowledge on to the coachee.

As a psychologist I work with senior managers in lots of different organisations, from finance to the law to retail and so on. They all know many things I do not. But I know a lot about what makes people tick. Sometimes I will share some of that knowledge with my coachees, if it is relevant, if they are interested.

Again, the role of teacher should be used sparingly. It is certainly ridiculous to avoid it, out of some kind of purist commitment to non-directive coaching. If the coach knows something that could help the coachee significantly, it is best to share that knowledge straightforwardly. Of course, the coach will say 'Look, this might not be relevant here' or 'I'm not sure how exactly this could work in your situation' and will make sure that teaching becomes mutual exploration as soon as possible. But it would be disrespectful to the coachee to sit there asking question after question when what you really think would be helpful is to tell him about something.

However, too much teaching encourages passivity in the coachee, and that is unlikely to be what he is looking for. The key is to be aware of when the coach has moved into a teaching role, and to ensure she moves out of it quickly. In the short term it can feel to both coach and coachee as if lots of progress is being made when the coach is doing lots of teaching. But in the long term, teaching is unlikely to be as effective as other roles in enabling the coachee to achieve his goals. And too much teaching can actually result in a deterioration in performance.

Mike Brearley, for example, knows a man who is an extremely keen cricket coach of young boys and girls. But whenever Mike sees this man, he is going down to the net to talk to them after virtually every ball. He will tell them things about every bit of their bodies, feet, legs,

weight, head, shoulder, elbow, hands, eyes. Mike says: 'He is like a cen-
tipede's coach who asks the centipede to focus on every move of every leg; and then is surprised when the centipede falls in the ditch at its first step.'

> *Too much teaching encourages passivity in the coachee, and that is unlikely to be what he is looking for. The key is to be aware of when the coach has moved into a teaching role, and to ensure she moves out of it quickly.*

Coach as 'safe container'

I struggled with what to call this role, and have ended up with a rather inelegant phrase. But it captures well what is going on.

Sometimes people have so much intense feeling that they cannot move beyond it. Typical feelings of this kind I have come across in my experience as coach are: anger at a boss's behaviour, disappointment at a setback, fear of a colleague, distress at the impact of a change in role, and many more. What people need is somewhere they can express those feelings, know that they have been heard, understood and taken seriously, and walk away in absolute confidence that their listener does not think any the less of them for what they have heard. (It goes without saying that they also need to be confident that what they have said will never be repeated.)

A coach can fulfil this role. It is very useful to the coachee, because it enables them to move on.

I remember a two-hour session with one very senior manager during which all he did was express his rage at the way the organisation had treated him (and in fact the organisation had treated him pretty disgracefully). I did nothing other than listen, explore and understand. I empathised too, and became angry myself at certain things he told me (but not in a way that distracted from his anger).

He was much less angry at the end of the session – what I mean is, his feelings were much less intense. But nothing else had changed. It was the last session I was due to have with him. I heard from him and about him subsequently. He made some decisions, sorted out some relationships, and found a role in the organisation he wanted and an exit path that worked both for him and his employers. This story is a classic example of how people need a 'safe container' to express strong feelings and to free themselves to move on.

Clearly, if the coach finds herself being used in this role almost continuously by a coachee, and strong feelings preventing progress are always the dominant theme of the sessions, then that may be an indication that counselling or therapy are what is needed rather than coaching. But in the vast majority of coaching relationships, if the coach can be a 'safe container' for a while, soon the coachee will be free of his intense feelings and keen to use his coach as sounding board, conscience, or teacher.

Coach as 'professional friend'

Most of the time I think the phrase 'professional friend' sums up quite well the dominant coaching role. It has two distinct types of meaning.

First, the 'professional friend' is a friend with a specific purpose. Unlike a general friend, the purpose of whose time with you is unplanned and just evolves, a coach has been given a particular job to do. She is to keep you company, think and feel with you, increase your sense of your own journey, as you plan to achieve your important goals.

Second, you know you can rely on your coach to behave professionally. She abides by rules and principles of conduct that lend security and formality to the 'friendship'.

But like a friend, your coach, in this role, is your equal. Like a friend, she wants the best for you. And like a friend, she shares your experience and increases your own awareness of your experience and your understanding of what you want to do next.

A final word on roles

The list of roles we have dealt with here is not intended to be exhaustive. Think, for example, of a coach as *mirror* (reflecting back to you what you are saying and doing, so you realise more clearly what it is), *celebrator* (enabling you to take stock of and enjoy your successes), *guru* (saying simple things that strike a chord and suddenly clarify something important), and so on and so on.

In a way, coaching is about moving between many different roles, limited only by the underlying ethic of coaching and the imagination of coach and coachee. The more aware both coach and coachee can be of the roles that are possible, and the roles that are actually in play at any time, and the more they can cultivate flexibility in roles, the more they will both get from the coaching relationship.

Chapter 11

Danger points

Introduction

In the last two chapters, we have touched on the risks that can arise at the start of and during a coaching relationship. In this chapter I want to look more explicitly at when the coaching relationship itself is most likely to be threatened, because of what is going on in it.

Now I do not think that it is a good thing for coaching relationships to last forever. They should last until the coachee has had as much help as he is likely to get from that coach with his important goals of the time. But I do think it is a bad thing if a coaching relationship breaks down. I think that almost always leaves both parties feeling uncomfortable, and it can get in the way of the coachee making progress with his goals and being able to benefit from coaching in the future.

So in this chapter, we identify three 'danger points', where the coach primarily, but also the coachee, need to be aware that if they aren't careful the relationship could be damaged.

The three human preoccupations

In their remarkably readable and insightful book *Difficult Conversations* (2000), Douglas Stone, Bruce Patton and Sheila Heen summarise the three essential questions about ourselves with which we are all and for all of our lives preoccupied. We ask ourselves:

- Am I competent?
- Am I a good person?
- Am I worthy of love?

We spend most of our lives trying to establish that the answer to each of these questions is 'yes'; we flourish when we get evidence that it is; and we are thrown into self-doubt and anxiety when we get evidence that the answer might be 'no'. We avoid people and situations that make us feel we might not be competent, or a good person or worthy of love.

The coaching relationship as it unfolds should provide to the coachee more certainty that his answers to these questions are 'yes'. But sometimes things happen during coaching that make him wonder if the coach is meaning 'no'. Those are the 'danger points' of this chapter.

Threats to competence

We have talked already about the way in which individuals' needs for control, and some of the 'power struggles' coach and coachee can get into, reflect a human preoccupation with feeling competent (see Chapter 9). Here we take this thinking a step further, because understanding the importance of these feelings is so important for coaches. For the very act of accepting a coach can threaten a coachee's belief that she is competent. She may have heard, or come to the view, 'competent people don't need coaching'. She may know that in the past coaching has been offered to poor performers in her organisation (see Chapter 1, on 'starting points' for coaching).

Unless this threat to something so important to a coachee's self-esteem can be countered, she is unlikely to be enthusiastic about the coaching process, or indeed the coach. Her coach will need to explain coaching in a way that restores confidence that it is indeed a process for competent people, and he will need to demonstrate his respect for his coachee's competence by the way he talks with her and deals with her.

But this threat, and the danger to the coaching relationship that it brings, can occur not just at the beginning but at any time in the process. When the coach challenges or teaches (see last chapter), the coachee may feel less competent herself. She may also feel that the coach is doing those things because he thinks she isn't so competent. In order to understand what the coach has to do to counter the threat, we need to look a little more closely at what it means to us to be 'competent'.

It has to do with whether we are valued for what we know and what we do, whether we are intelligent and capable people. Different people will have different measures that matter to them. For a mother, she may derive a sense of her competence from the behaviour and adjustment of her children. For an academic, it may be her position in a university and the reputation of her research. For a businesswoman, it may be the profitability of her business. For many of us, salary and status are two important measures of competence, and that is why we get agitated about drops in either of these.

But little things can trigger anxieties about competence. A coachee of mine was an appalling speller. He still took his spelling mistakes seriously, even though he was hugely successful at work. I once pointed out a mistake in something he had written; I sensed immediately (using my early warning system – see Chapter 9) that I had caused a problem in our relationship. I vowed never to correct his spelling again; it wasn't necessary.

But we have seen that coaches do have to challenge sometimes, when that is the most helpful thing for our coachees. We need to be alert to the reaction of our coachee. We need to make it clear that we are challenging a specific view, or action, not their competence as a whole. We need to resist challenging more than the coachee can bear. To do so is useless. If he accepts a challenge that leaves him feeling incompetent, that will disempower him. If he rejects us, because we are damaging his self-esteem, that may damage the coaching relationship irreparably.

This is where respect comes in again (Chapter 4). So long as a coach feels respectful towards her coachee, she is probably not going to make him doubt his competence for very long.

Threats to goodness

The need to feel that we are 'good' is about being confident that our contribution to others is positive. It is about not hurting people intentionally, about caring for others, meaning well, doing some good. Whenever we hurt someone else, we become anxious about this. That is one of the reasons why it is hard to break up with a partner even if it is you doing the breaking.

Coaches have to be careful in relation to this need in their coachees. Because of the nature of the coaching relationship, a coachee may feel her coach knows her better than almost anyone else. If she gets the slightest hint that the coach might be judging her to be 'a bad person', it will therefore matter far more than if, say, her boss suggested she was. 'What does he know?' she might say, and 'He only thinks that because I don't do what he wants.' But her coach is in a privileged position.

So coaches must do two things. They must ensure they are not passing judgment on their coachees' 'goodness'. They need to stick firmly to the view that 'people do the best they can at the time'. If something looks malicious or cruel, so be it. It is not possible to know another person's full intentions. The coach's job is to help the coachee explore and understand the consequences of his actions, not pass judgments on his intentions.

Should a coach come to a view that a coachee is not a 'good' person in the sense we are talking about here, he should stop working with her. How could he help her achieve her goals, if that were the case?

The second thing coaches must do is be careful when talking with coachees about anything to do with their motives. Even a casual remark such as 'I guess you wanted to get even' could worry the coachee. It will, as we have said already, be important to the coachee to be sure their coach considers them a 'good' person.

> The coach's job is to help the coachee explore and understand the consequences of his actions, not pass judgments on his intentions.

Threats to love

People often get very uncomfortable when the word 'love' is used in a work context. It seems too personal, too intimate. But human beings are looking for love the whole time. At work we call it 'acceptance', 'recognition' and 'valuing'.

Again, a coach is in a privileged position, because she knows the coachee better than most. So she must ensure she does not damage his sense of his own 'lovableness' – or 'value'. That is why it is very important for coaches to keep appointments and only change them for very good reasons. That is why it is important to agree at the outset of coaching when and how it will end. That is why a coach should not work with someone she does not care about.

TOOLS AND
TECHNIQUE

Introduction

Salvador Minuchin is one of the most well-respected family therapists in the world. Like Carl Rogers (see Chapter 6), Minuchin could enable people to change the course of their lives in a conversation. His work is relevant to this book because you could see him as a 'coach' of families. Among other things, he enabled families to achieve their goals, and individuals within those families to achieve their goals, through helping them discover more choices and do things differently.

What Minuchin has to say about 'techniques' is particularly relevant to Part Four of this book. He wrote that the use of the word 'techniques' (which was part of the title of one of his most widely read books (1981)) did imply good things such as craftsmanship, and attention to detail. But it also can suggest images of people manipulating other people. 'Spectres of brainwashing, or control for the sake of personal power, hover.' Minuchin expressed sympathy with such concerns.

He also pointed out that technique alone does not guarantee effectiveness. If a coach comes to rely too heavily and too consciously on technique, she will remain a craftsman; while she may be very 'professional', her contact with her coachees may also be rather superficial.

Minuchin's point is that over-use, and over-conscious use, of tools and technique detracts from one person's focus on and respect for another. His recommendation is that techniques should only be learned in order, ultimately, to be forgotten.

I agree with him. I have myself sometimes suggested to a coachee we 'try something out', and seen their face fall. At that moment, they sensed that my absolute attention to them had been disrupted by my interest in the application of some technique. So that is why this part of the book comes at this relatively late stage.

Unless tools and techniques are used in the context of all we have said in Parts One, Two and Three, they are at best useless, at worst destructive. But if they are used within the context of a coaching relationship such as we have described so far, they can be sources of creativity, of clarity and ultimately of change.

In this part of the book, we describe different kinds of work the coach and coachee do together. We give practical guidelines on how to do this work effectively, including tools, techniques, frameworks and formats that we have found helpful to our coachees. Hopefully, these chapters provide some structure to the free-flowing, dynamic and complex process called 'coaching'. Hopefully, too, they provide techniques that coaches can learn and then 'forget' – in other words, techniques that fit so well with the style of the coach and the relationship of coach and coachee that they form a natural part of the work.

That means, of course, that not every technique is usable by every coach; it is important to learn only those techniques that you feel entirely comfortable with.

Chapter 12

Building rapport

Introduction

Rapport needs to be established at the start of a coaching relationship, but not only then. It needs to be re-established at the start of every session, and when something has happened in a session that breaks the rapport between coach and coachee (see the last chapter on 'danger points' in the coaching relationship; at all these points, rapport may be broken).

We have talked at some length already in this book about the importance of safety in a coaching relationship. The concept of rapport is closely related to that. Rapport is there when we feel we have nothing to fear from the other person, and they feel the same about us. When two people first meet, there is almost always a mix of pleasure and apprehension. Once rapport has been established, the apprehension has gone.

My favourite definition of 'rapport' is 'mutual recognition and respect'. The 'recognition' happens as people exchange information about themselves to each other, both explicitly and implicitly. Once I feel that I know what to expect from you, I begin to feel comfortable. (So long as you remain a puzzle or a mystery, I can't be sure you won't harm me.) But for rapport, recognition alone is not enough. There must be respect (as we have defined it in Chapter 4, where we also describe how respect is necessary for a coachee to feel safe). If you don't respect me, you might try to change or control me.

> Rapport is there when we feel we have nothing to fear from the other person, and they feel the same about us.

Clearly, initial rapport is different from the deep rapport experienced by two colleagues who have enjoyed working together for years. So rapport is developing, or diminishing, all the time, and it is an important part of our work as coaches to develop it.

What tools, and what technique, can help us in this aspect of our work?

Paying attention to physical reactions

We touched on this in Chapter 9, where we explored how to recognise mismatches in the coaching relationship. We pointed out that we feel in our own bodies when something is awry in a relationship. I want to take this a little further here, because paying attention to our own and other people's physical reactions can be a very helpful technique in building rapport.

When rapport is broken, there is danger for us. It might be the danger of loss of self-esteem, as someone we wanted to associate with rejects us. It might be the danger of embarrassment, as we fail to communicate clearly. It might be the danger of conflict or of being forced to do something we don't want to.

We all have physical responses to danger that are characteristic of us. One of mine, for example, is a prickling sensation on the backs of my hands. A colleague of mine sweats profusely. Another finds his mouth goes dry.

If we can learn to notice these changes, they carry useful information. They tell us when rapport is being built, and when it is being broken. Also, the more we pay attention to our own physical reactions, the more likely we are to notice those of others. And as we all know, there is far more information exchanged between people on this nonverbal level than with words – particularly information related to rapport.

The parts of our bodies that are most likely to carry and communicate this kind of information are those connected to our 'fight or flight' capabilities. So, skin colour and body temperature are often good sources of information, as the blood supply to different parts of our body is altered in response to a real or imagined threat. You might feel hot (or cold); you might see someone flush (or go pale). Sensations in the skin (like my prickling hands) are due to the same mechanism.

Our digestive system is another good source of information. You might feel 'butterflies'; you might see another person bend slightly to ease a feeling of discomfort in her stomach.

Trembles and quavering in movement and voice are other common signs, as are 'defensive' or uncomfortable-looking body positions – it is as if we are getting ready for action.

Facial expression is also informative. After all, our faces are designed to warn off and welcome others. It is amazing to me how often people will ignore the information contained in others' facial expressions. They will certainly have noticed a frown, a blink, a smile or a 'moue', but they often don't appear to use the information such expressions contain. I have observed many meetings, for example, where the speaker continues on a particular track in apparent ignorance of the frowns and wandering eyes of his colleagues.

It is important to remember that people can be very idiosyncratic, particularly when it comes to their physical response to a psychological rather than a physical threat. So there is no straightforward 'rule book' to interpret the signs.

(A coach I know thought she was never going to build rapport with one particular woman, because this woman frowned during most of the first coaching session. It transpired that the coachee was in considerable pain because of a hernia, and her frown had nothing to do with the coach and everything to do with trying to control the pain!)

The technique is not about following a rule book but rather about getting to know your own physical reactions, and becoming more aware of all the physical changes in others. Such awareness will not give you the ability to 'read others' minds'. But it will add a whole new stream of information that is of great relevance to the work of building rapport. Good coaches use this information constantly.

I remember a colleague of mine, for example, describing how he noticed his coachee's eyes flick away whenever he mentioned her boss. He pondered this, and suddenly remembered that it was her boss who had recommended him as coach for this woman. He wondered if she was uncomfortable with his relationship with her boss, and if as a consequence she wasn't sure where he, her coach, was 'coming from'.

In the following session, he discussed at greater length with her the groundrules and boundaries of his coaching relationship with her, and clarified that once coaching had started there was complete confidentiality, and absolute focus on her goals and interests. She then began to talk about a serious issue she had with her boss that she needed to resolve.

Now, maybe she would have come to that point anyway. But I believe my colleague's attentiveness to her physical responses, and the action he took as a result of the information he gained, was instrumental in building rapport so that she could raise an issue that felt 'dangerous' to her.

Every time rapport needs to be established or re-established, we should increase our level of attentiveness to our own and our coachee's physical responses. At the start of every session, for example, notice how our coachee looks. And how do we feel as we greet her? For we shall be reacting unconsciously to the 'mood' she has brought with her.

The 'first question'

In building rapport, as in so many things, 'well begun is half-done'. Also, it is very hard work to recover from a bad beginning. So when rapport has to be established or re-established we need as much information as possible about the other person, so that we can show through our subsequent actions that we have recognised where they are, and respect them wherever that may be.

What we need is a tool for enabling them to reveal that information. And that tool is 'the first question'. I call it the 'first question' because it is a beginning (of a journey of exploration into the other person's world), and because it often turns out to be the most important question you ask in a whole session.

There is no single 'first question'. You need to find 'first questions' that fit your style (and of course do not jar with your coachee). I know a coach who begins many sessions by asking 'What ails?' Few of us could use a question like that naturally, but it works for him. I know another who often asks 'Are you having fun?' Again, it works for him. I am most likely to ask vague questions such as 'What's been going on?', 'How are things?' and 'What's new?'

There is some merit in having an open question of this type, which is an 'old friend' and which both you and your coachees recognise as a sign that you are in totally active listening mode, with nothing else on your mind than interest in where your coachee is.

There is no single 'first question'. You need to find 'first questions' that fit your style (and of course do not jar with your coachee).

I do not call it the 'first question' because it always comes first in a session. It often does – but it is useful at any point where you feel you need more information about what your coachee is really thinking and feeling, in other words, when you sense rapport needs to be strengthened.

The six levels of rapport

It can be useful to have a framework in your mind that ensures that you don't neglect any of the levels at which rapport can be built and broken. The framework I have in my mind is derived from an NLP ('neuro-linguistic programming') model called 'logical levels'. I call it 'psychological levels', because that means more to me, and it is reproduced in Figure 1.

= where someone is, literally; the places and physical contexts in which he/she exists and operates

= what someone does

= skills, what someone is capable of

= fundamental principles and perceptions that someone holds about life and how it should be lived, eg 'from each according to his ability, to each according to his needs'; 'do unto others as you would be done by'

= who someone believes him/herself to be, eg 'I'm a tough MD'; 'I'm a caring father'; 'I'm a loyal friend'

= our connection with the universe and with humankind generally

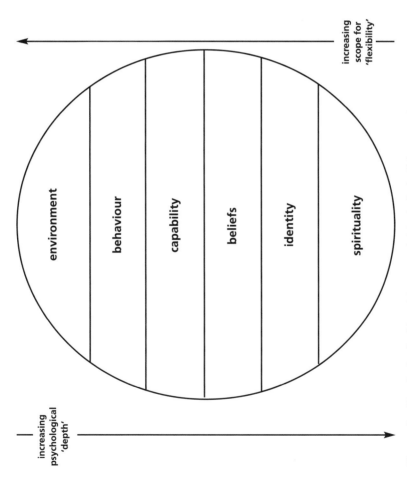

increasing scope for 'flexibility'

environment

behaviour

capability

beliefs

identity

spirituality

increasing psychological 'depth'

Figure 1 *'Psychological levels' – a model to help build rapport*

The framework draws our attention to the fact that we are always processing information at a number of levels simultaneously. All these levels represent rapport-building opportunities, and also of course rapport-breaking risks.

On the 'top' level, we are processing information about our 'environment'. We are physical beings, as we have just been discussing, and our physical state matters to us. If someone causes us physical discomfort, rapport will be damaged; conversely if someone attends to our physical needs in an appropriate way, that can be a first step to good rapport. Also, environments mean different things to different people, and if we can respond to that it will be helpful.

A coachee of mine visited me in the offices of the company I worked for. Previously, all our sessions had been at his office. At the end of the session he said: 'The décor of these offices is all wrong. I expected something much softer and more welcoming. All these black leather chairs and shiny surfaces are off-putting.' He was almost cross with me for conducting a coaching session with him in such an environment. Rapport was definitely shaken.

Then we come to the level of 'behaviour'. Every aspect of our behaviour may show recognition of and respect for our coachee, or fail to. From the way we greet her to the way we take notes to the way we set up sessions; from the clothes we wear to the accent we speak with to the amount we smile – we are building or breaking rapport. So we need to remember that if we detect signs (by paying attention as we discussed in the last section) that rapport is dented, it could be the result of something quite easy to change.

At the level of 'capability', rapport will be built as we demonstrate that we have the skills appropriate to the coaching relationship. We are moving to deeper and more enduring levels of rapport here, but they take longer to establish. If rapport is damaged too much in the early and more superficial stages, we may never get the chance to demonstrate our skill.

Once we arrive at the much deeper levels of 'beliefs', 'identity' and 'spirituality' we have the most powerful opportunities to build and break rapport. We need to pay close attention to the information we gain as we spend more time with our coachees about what matters to them at these levels.

One of the reasons that we as coaches need the beliefs and values we described in Chapter 4 is that those are the beliefs and values that are most likely to build rapport at these deeper levels with the widest range of people.

We do not sit down with our coachees and say 'Now we need to do some rapport-building'. But it is an essential and constant part of our work with them, and they would expect us to do it.

A very dissatisfied coachee talked to me recently about a coach who failed to do this work properly (and whom he rapidly 'sacked'). She insisted on coming to his home for the first session (he keeps his home life and work life very separate); she sent him e-mails between sessions, which he did not see the point of; and she gave him 'two things to think about while you're on the beach' when he was about to go on a much-needed holiday (and remember, he likes to keep home and work separate!). It beggars belief how she managed to miss the signs and break rapport so comprehensively.

I use the 'psychological levels' as a permanent mental reminder to myself that rapport is at the heart of good coaching.

Chapter 13

Setting goals

Introduction

We said right at the start of this book that 'A coach is someone who helps another person ... articulate and achieve their goals.' So it is clear that articulating goals is an important part of the work a coach and a coachee must do together. In fact, the key difference between people who do achieve their goals and people who don't is that people who do, know what their goals are. So if a coach can help a coachee articulate her goals, she will be in all likelihood be more than half-way to achieving them.

Also, it is important for the coaching relationship as a whole, and indeed each individual session, to have goals that are clearly articulated and agreed by coach and coachee. That does not mean that coaching is always governed by a 'SMART' goal (see below) – different coachees need different kinds of goals at different times (see the section later in this chapter on a framework for understanding individual differences in goal-setting). But it does mean that as much of the time as possible coach and coachee should have a shared idea in their minds of what they are trying to achieve.

It sounds straightforward. But in fact it is the most difficult thing in the world. Deciding what we really want, that is the hard thing. Getting what we want is easy by comparison. So what tools, and what technique, can a coach draw on to assist in this most difficult of work?

There is one more thing that needs to be said before we look at tools and technique – and it is fundamental. We might think that setting goals is the first thing that is done in a programme of coaching, and then once the goals are clear we move on to the next stage. But a few minutes of reflection on coaching we have given or received will immediately put us right. The process of becoming clear about what we want is a process that continues throughout coaching. We not only clarify and refine what we know about our goals, we change them.

Right now, for example, I am coaching a senior manager who was originally focused on increasing her influence with her superiors in her current position. Now after several months she has come to the view that she needs a change of role. That is now her priority. Who knows how things will develop next?

This kind of evolution of goals is the norm, not the exception. So underlying everything that we shall now say about tools and technique in goal-setting is the fundamental principle that these tools and this technique need to be applied fluidly, dynamically and continuously, not as discrete interventions.

A goal-setting 'process'

What we have just said applies particularly to the 'goal-setting process' I am about to describe. It is a good process because it alerts us to all the kinds of thinking a coachee needs to do around her goals, and it guides the coach to interventions that will encourage each kind of thinking. But it would be rare that a coach would take a coachee through the whole process step by step. What the coach will do more usually is keep a sense of which thinking has been done and which has not, and of which thinking is most important right now. The framework of 'process' helps her do that.

The stages of the process are these (and where I use the word 'articulate', it may be either coach or coachee doing the actual articulating, but of course the coachee is the one who says whether the articulation is right):

- *Diagnose* From exploration of what has brought the coachee to coaching, articulate a general sense of what she wants to achieve
- *Be positive* Check the goal is positively stated (as something to move towards, not as something to move away from; to 'start' doing something new, not 'stop' doing something, for example)
- *Check commitment* Explore how the coachee knows she wants to achieve this: what's the evidence? How does she usually know when she wants something? Does this fit? Is she sure she wants it for herself, or is it something others want her to achieve?
- *Think systemically* Explore the broader context: what effects will achieving this goal have? What effects on others, as well as the coachee? How will others react?

- *Check control* Explore whether it is within the coachee's power to achieve this goal: what things are likely to hinder her? How could she get control over these things? Is she assuming other people will change? Does she have the skills, abilities and other personal qualities she needs to achieve this goal? Can she acquire them? Does she have the time and the energy?
- *Assess value* Explore whether the goal is worth the effort it will take: how much effort will it be? What will be the pay-off? Is it a 'leveraged' goal? Does it result in other desirable things being achieved, as side-effects or direct consequences?
- *Get specific* Explore how achievement of the goal can be 'measured': how will she know the goal has been achieved? How will others know? Is the goal clearly expressed? Could she explain it to others?
- *Rediagnose* Explore whether her sense of what she wants to achieve has changed as a consequence of thinking it through: are there other things that now seem more of a priority? Have subgoals emerged? How is she feeling about this goal right now?
- *Test reality* Using all the information that has been generated, articulate the goal that now makes sense to the coachee.

A person who has been helped to think in all these ways about what she really wants is likely to be either sure she knows or sure she doesn't know. Either is a good outcome, and enables her to move forward – either to planning or to a journey of self-exploration.

The 'right-brain question'

The goal-setting process we have just described is on the whole a left-brain analytical approach. As coaches, we need to work with both left brain and right brain, whichever can furnish our coachees with more resources to achieve their goals. To elicit the help of the right brain (the more imaginative side of our brain, and the side more concerned with emotion), we can ask the following question:

> 'Imagine it is next Monday/next week/a year from today (choose a time scale that seems appropriate). You have achieved your goal and you are now able to (describe the outcome). How are you feeling?'

In order to answer this question, a coachee has first of all to imagine herself in the future. This alone begins to 'wake up' the right side of the brain. Then she has to imagine in some detail what the world is like for her, now she has achieved her goal. The simple act of imagining success makes success more likely, for it sets in train right-brain processes that are directed towards making that vision come true. Finally, it is feelings not reasons that provide the vast majority of our driving force. So by accessing and engaging feelings connected with the goal, the coachee increases her commitment to it and energy for planning.

The 'right-brain question' may lead into a whole new conversation about goals, as well as provide some extra information and energy in connection with a goal already articulated. It is best asked when a coachee has come to the end of analysis, and feels that her reality is well understood.

In brief solution-focused therapy (a therapy with many similarities to coaching as it proceeds by solving specific problems and not by a deep exploration of an individual's psychological make-up), this kind of question is known as 'the miracle question'. It is slightly different in form, but again it encourages right-brain thinking to get clarity about what you really want. The miracle question goes like this:

> 'Imagine it is tomorrow morning and a miracle has happened overnight. You are now in the position you always wanted to be, your problems are solved and you are happy. What has changed? In you, in those around you, in your circumstances?'

I asked the right-brain question recently of a coachee who had as his primary goal leaving corporate life in two years' time. I said: 'Imagine it is two years from today and you have left. You are secure about your finances, and happy that you have finished the work you set out to do in corporate life. It is the first day of the rest of your life. How do you feel?'

He closed his eyes (another good way to calm down the left brain and wake up the right), and went quiet for a minute or two. I watched as an expression of real joy came over his face. He opened his eyes and said 'I need to achieve this in one year, not two – and I think I know how.'

Such is the power of the right brain.

A framework for understanding individual differences in goal-setting

However good a goal-setting process is, it won't work for everyone. That is because people have very different preferences when it comes to setting goals for themselves. Here is a framework that identifies some of the important differences, and helps us adapt the goal-setting work we do to suit different coachees.

People can be classified into four types when it comes to their approach to goal-setting (Richard Boyatzis, personal communication, 2000).

- About 40 per cent of us are 'objectives-oriented planners'. A typical plan for us would be: 'I'd like to be in Manchester by 9 am tomorrow.' We like to have a fairly specific articulation of a goal but don't need or want all the steps to that goal defined. We like our coach to help us set 'SMART' goals (ie Specific, Measurable, Achievable but challenging, Relevant, and Time-bound).
- A further 40 per cent of us are 'domain and direction planners'. A typical plan for us would be: 'I'd like to get to Manchester soon.' We like our coach to help us achieve a sense of direction but are not hugely interested in tying ourselves down to a particular end-state.
- About 15 per cent of us are 'action planners'. We say: 'Tomorrow I will get up at 8, and catch the 10.15 train to Manchester.' We like our coach to help us make action plans that we can commit to, but we don't feel the need to articulate goals as such.
- A small but significant 5 per cent of us are 'existentialists'. We find ourselves on a train for some reason, and end up getting off at Manchester. We don't plan consciously. We find out what we want by inference, from what we end up doing. We like our coach to help us reflect on the consequences and implications of what we're doing.

'Ideal self' exercises

Developmental goals result from an awareness of a gap between who we are and who we would like to be. Often what people need most help with is working out who they want to be, in other words, articulating their 'ideal self'. As a coach, we can help them with exercises such as these:

List '27 things I'd like to do or experience before I die'.

If you won five million pounds, how would your life and work change?

If you were living your ideal life in 2015, what would a video show as it recorded a week in your life?

These three exercises are powerful, but people need time to do them. Often the best thing is to suggest they do them before the next session, and then you can talk together about what emerged. What does the response tell your coachee about how he would like to be living and working? Is he living and working in that way now?

Other useful 'ideal self questions' are:

- Whom do you admire? Who are role models for you?
- When are you most proud of yourself?
- What are your worst of times/best of times?
- What legacy would you like to leave in the world of work?

Questions such as these have to be part of a journey of self-exploration that a coachee has explicitly welcomed. They cannot be suddenly introduced, nor should they be forced on people. They can only be effective when they are a response to a coachee's state of mind, and to his interest in finding out more about what he really wants.

Chapter 14

Developing
self-awareness

Introduction

In exploring the work of setting goals, the last chapter was concerned with an aspect of self-awareness – knowing what one wants. But there are many other aspects of self-awareness that can be developed, and this is an important part of the work we do as coaches.

In fact, some people would say it is the most important part of that work. The current research into emotional intelligence and its impact on success in all areas of work (and indeed outside work) places self-awareness at the heart of effectiveness (see, for example, Daniel Goleman's books such as *Working with Emotional Intelligence* (1998) and Rob Goffee and Gareth Jones's research (2000) at London Business School into what makes people effective leaders). Will Schutz (whose model of human social needs we explained and used in Chapter 9) wrote the following in 1994 after decades of work with people in organisations:

'The new consciousness that is needed to solve many personal, professional, international, and organisational problems is, I believe, self-consciousness or self-awareness, which is directly related to self-esteem.'

He goes on to elaborate, as many have done before and since, that when a person knows and accepts themselves, they are able to be fully productive and to build productive relationships with others.

I have found in my many years of coaching that it is increased self-awareness that coachees most value, and which produces the most long-lasting and positive change for them.

Increased self-awareness is not the same as feedback. Feedback can lead to an increase in self-awareness, but it often doesn't. That is because an increase in self-awareness, as the word itself makes clear, is about a change that happens inside someone. Feedback may stay on the 'outside'; I have seen individuals ignore totally very 'accurate' feedback because they suspected the intentions of the giver, or doubted the relevance of the feedback to their own goals, or couldn't bear the pain of accepting it to be true.

It is in a coaching relationship, with all the underpinning ground rules, values and norms of behaviour that we have described in Parts One, Two and Three of this book, that an individual can be enabled to take stock of all the 'feedback' she has received over the years, and take it inside herself, and so develop her awareness of herself.

How can her coach help her do that?

Diagnostic tools

There are a great many psychometric and pseudo-psychometric instruments available. From fully researched instruments that can only be used by qualified professionals (such as the Myers–Briggs Type Indicator® – see Chapter 3) to quick questionnaires anyone can access in books or on the Internet (such as Seligman's 'Signature Strengths Survey' and Landsberg's 'coaching self-assessment'), just about any aspect of personality, behaviour, ability and preference can be 'measured' in some way. Then there is 360-degree feedback, which, used in the right context, is an invaluable tool for people who want to understand better the impact of their behaviour on their key relationships at work.

These kinds of diagnostic tools can be good starting points for a conversation that will lead to an increase in self-awareness. Psychometric questionnaires allow people to 'benchmark' themselves against others.

I have known people discover that, for example, although they always assumed they were particularly shy, it could well be that they 'aren't much shyer than average', and, conversely, I have known people discover an 'extreme' trait, which they had not until then realised was remarkable in comparison to others.

> *Diagnostic tools can be good starting points for a conversation that will lead to an increase in self-awareness. Psychometric questionnaires allow people to 'benchmark' themselves against others.*

Also, all the questionnaires can provide a focus, and a structure, for a journey of self-discovery. It is hard for any of us to take a blank sheet of paper and 'describe ourselves' (although some coaches incorporate just such an exercise into their work). The diagnostic tools help us get started. Also, they often draw a coachee's attention to precisely those aspects of himself that are likely to be particularly significant in determining his success or failure. 360-degree feedback questionnaires, for example, will typically be structured round the competencies most relevant to the role the recipient of the feedback has.

All the diagnostics need a lot of interpretation, though. And I do not just mean the professional interpretation a qualified practitioner can give. I am not just talking about psychometric measures here.

What I mean is interpretation from data to information. In other words, I am talking about the work that allows a recipient of feedback to work out what it all means to him. Only when that work has been done can there be the possibility of an increase in self-awareness.

Let me illustrate this central point with two examples, one from a psychometric context and one from a 360-degree context.

A coachee of mine took a 'big five' personality questionnaire (one that measures aspects of the five fundamental personality traits – extraversion, anxiety, agreeableness, openness to experience, and conscientiousness). She found she had a very low score on 'straightforwardness': in other words, the questionnaire suggested that she could be manipulative in her dealings with others.

At first we could not make sense of this. It did not accord with her preference for plain speaking at work (and it did not accord with my experience of her as my coachee). After some discussion, she realised that the relationship she had had uppermost in her mind when she answered those questions was her relationship with her disabled and rather unpredictable husband, where for some very good reasons she often found herself being quite 'canny' in her communications with him.

At that point the score in the questionnaire made sense to her, and she began to explore the consequences of this communication pattern with her husband not only for her relationship with him but for her relationships at work. She reflected that there were certain situations in which her capacity for slightly devious communication was triggered, and she spent some time analysing where that happens and whether she wanted to change her behaviour.

Now, had she never taken that diagnostic questionnaire, this aspect of her style might never have emerged, and she would not have had the opportunity to increase her self-awareness in that respect. But had the questionnaire not been 'interpreted' through conversation and reflection, she would have been both unable and unwilling to make any use of that information at all.

Now let's look briefly at the 360-degree example. Another coachee of mine was struggling in a highly 'political' environment, which was causing him a great deal of stress. He often said how much he hated those kinds of politics, preferring a more open, honest and achievement-oriented atmosphere at work.

In a 360-degree exercise he completed during this time, a couple of comments were made that he was 'too political'. His first reaction was to discount these comments as coming from two specific individuals who didn't like or trust him. But I encouraged him to think a bit more about this point, and to try to work out if there was any other meaning behind it.

We explored the possibility that he was beginning to operate a policy of 'if you can't beat them, join them' and to move away from his naturally open style to a style he was far less skilled at: the style of the political 'operator'. He recognised some truth in that, and began to reflect on what he was doing and what the effects were. His self-awareness had increased, but again, only because he had the time, space and, most importantly, safety, to interpret the feedback.

So to summarise the points I have made about diagnostic tools:

- they can be a useful starting point for developing self-awareness
- to be useful, there must be extensive 'interpretation' of the raw data they provide
- 'interpretation' means the active exploration by the coachee, with the coach's help, of what he 'makes of' the data
- the coaching environment is an ideal environment for such interpretation to take place, because it provides time, support, and psychological safety.

Listening to the coachee's story

Of all the tools and all the techniques for developing an individual's self-awareness, listening to their story is my favourite. (I am taking it for granted that the coach is listening in the way we described in Chapter 6, so I am not going to repeat how the coach should be listening. Here I want to focus on what she is listening to.)

Of course, the coachee has many stories to tell. (There is no intention in my use of the word 'story' to imply fiction. My intention is to emphasise the personal and human nature of such accounts.) There is the story of how he came to coaching (see Chapter 1), the story of previous coaches he has known, the story of the issue he is bringing to the table, and so on. But the story I want to start with is the most important and all-encompassing story of all: it is the story he tells about his life.

Now that is not the same as the story a biographer would tell about his life. The coachee chooses what to include, he decides what is important and what is not; he makes a judgment about what would be interesting and informative for me, his coach, to hear. For that reason, I like to leave people free to tell their story in their own way.

One coachee of mine took the whole two hours of the first meeting, and he had only got to the age of sixteen. He still related much of his present behaviour back to childhood experiences that had made him, and still make him, very angry. Another told me her 'whole' story in twenty minutes! She was keen to live every day for itself, and didn't look back much.

I invite people to tell me their story quite straightforwardly: 'Tell me your story – where you began, how you came to be here, what the journey was.'

People don't often have the chance to tell their stories in this unhurried way. They listen to themselves more carefully, because their coach is listening. On more occasions than I could count, a coachee has said 'I never realised' (and he will mention some characteristic of himself or his life that emerged in the story) 'until today.' He will make connections between past experiences and present ones, between how he behaved as a child and how he behaves now. He will talk about key relationships, and relate it to things that matter to him now in relationships.

And he will, simply for hearing himself tell his own story, have an increased sense of himself, and of his distinctiveness. He will also most likely experience an increase in acceptance of himself – which is, paradoxically, a prerequisite for changing something about oneself. (If we don't accept ourselves, too much energy is spent defending against the attacks we imagine will come, and there isn't enough left for the creative act of change.) He will gain this increase in self-acceptance because of the nature of this kind of personal story-telling – no one is criticising or judging, both coach and coachee are simply wanting to hear.

Once the story has been told in the coaching context, it is always there as a resource. So all of the information contained in the facts of the story and in the manner of its telling continue to be in coach and coachee's minds when they meet. Here is just one of many examples of this, and of its positive effects in developing self-awareness.

I was working with a manager who had told as part of his story that he had been the 'peace-maker' in the family he had grown up in, a family full of warring elements and strong personalities. A few sessions later, he was bemoaning the fact that he didn't express his views more strongly at board meetings, but rather tried to help others achieve consensus.

At the moment of articulating this, he realised the connection – because he had told his story in my presence, in that room. He then went on to reflect on his patterns of behaviour that continued the pattern of peace-making, and to realise that it wasn't necessarily what the other board members wanted from him.

Because our values, beliefs and sense of who we are in the world have their roots in our early experiences, listening to a coachee's story in the sense I have just described it provides a huge amount of information about those most important aspects of her. The coach can help this information emerge, by listening for and reflecting back things the coachee says about what was important in her family of origin, what she was known for even as a child, what her hopes and dreams were, and so on.

When a coachee tells his story, he is giving himself feedback, and feedback at a level that is truly useful. The most useful feedback we get from others is often feedback that is very behavioural – 'when you do this, the reports you write go down well with the client'; 'when you do that, some of your staff don't have enough clarity', and so on.

But the most useful feedback we give ourselves is feedback that answers the question 'why?' – it is feedback that tells us how it has come to be that we behave in certain ways and not others. Once we feel we understand why (as we often do through

> The most useful feedback we get from others is often feedback that is very behavioural.

telling our story), we can make a decision about whether it feels right and safe to change. Feedback becomes an increase in self-awareness we can use, rather than data we feel unconnected to.

It is not always appropriate to ask a coachee to tell their story at the beginning of a coaching relationship. (Sometimes it isn't appropriate at all: for example, the coaching agenda is very specific, the coachee is very clear about the kind of help she wants from her coach, and it doesn't include a journey of self-exploration.) Often, as the coaching relationship develops, and increasing levels of trust are built, the coachee wants to tell more of his story. The coach needs to be alert to this, and give the coachee that space, because whenever a coachee wants to tell his story, an increase in self-awareness becomes very likely.

One last thing needs to be said about listening to other people's stories in a coaching, rather than a therapeutic, context. It is not the job of the coach to help heal emotional wounds in the coachee's past, or to help her mend relationships with family members. Sometimes such therapeutic effects will happen as a consequence of someone having told their story, but that will be something the coachee decides to do for herself.

If it emerges that the coachee wants to work with someone on these kinds of issues, then she will need to do so with an appropriately qualified therapist. The coach is listening to the coachee's story in order to develop the coachee's self-awareness and increase her resourcefulness to solve problems at work in the present. I know this distinction is not an easy one to make, but it is possible to make it, and it is important.

Exploring and understanding the coachee's role

A colleague of mine who is an excellent and experienced coach calls his coaching practice 'role counselling'. This name reflects the view that the idea that a person has in their mind of their role at work and the relationship they have with that idea have a fundamental impact on their effectiveness in their role. Notice that we are talking about 'the idea in their mind', and not about a procedural 'role definition'. It is ideas in our minds that affect our behaviour and feelings profoundly, not words on a piece of paper.

It follows that it is important to develop a coachee's self-awareness in this respect too. In other words, a coach can be very useful when he enables a coachee to become clearer about what she conceives her role to be and what she feels about it.

The sorts of questions a coach can ask to help a coachee get this kind of clarity are given in the accompanying box (I am indebted to Dr Richard Jones of Oxford Consulting for this particular set of questions).

> *Your external environment (deals with the broader global context in which your organisation exists)*
> - What is your understanding of the developments in the environment with which you are confronted – economic developments,

technological developments, social developments (are you in touch with generation shifts, social liberation movements, understanding cultures?), political developments?
- What influence has your work on your family and vice versa?
- What influence has your social environment (urban/rural, social class, and membership of professional/social/religious organisations, etc) had on your work and vice versa?

Your past
- With what background experience/expectations did you come to this organisation?
- How were you introduced, received, into the organisation?
- How has your career progressed to date? Have your expectations been met?
- What have been your most important successes, and what have been the setbacks?
- What have you learned from these?

Your current work
- What are your most important tasks?
- What are the different roles you take?
- How much of your job is: administrative/technical/specialist; advisory or consultative; teaching or developing others; policy, planning, long-term decision-making; developing yourself; other activities?
- What is the balance between these activities, and is it appropriate?
- What part of your work is stimulating and what boring?
- What changes would you like to make to your current work?
- Who does your job when you are away?

Your team
- What is the balance of skills and personalities in your team?
- How is conflict handled in your team?
- What is the climate in the team – is it constructive or are there problems you need to resolve?
- What are the systems and procedures your team has for carrying out its work?
- What are the mechanisms your team has for reviewing its process?
- What are the relationships your team has with other parts of the organisation?
- Are you comfortable with your team leadership?
- What are the opportunities you can see that will improve your team effectiveness and the team's effectiveness?

Your job experience (includes the people with whom you relate in the broader organisation, the organisational climate, the norms and values in as much as they stimulate or constrain your interests and endeavours)

- Through your job, what influence can you have on the character of the organisation?
- How would you describe the informal organisation chart – to show the key relationships that affect the way the organisation works?
- How would you describe your relationship with superiors/ colleagues/ subordinates?
- Do the standards and principles by which you work appear to be generated from within the organisation or outside it?
- From whom do you expect co-operation and support? Who can you count on?
- Who are the people you could regard as mentors, the ones with whom you can discuss important issues?
- Are you having enough fun at work?

Your future (based on taking stock of the past and present, a thoughtful look into the future as to where your life is taking you)

- How do you see your career developing?
- How do you see the future of the organisation and your evolving role in this?
- What are the gaps between the way the organisation presently functions and how you believe it should function?
- What do you need to do to create the future you desire?

In many ways, this line of questioning is another kind of listening to the coachee's story, and specifically the story of her role. It has all the potential benefits we explored in the last section.

The 'morning pages'

In her book *The Artist's Way* (1992), Julia Cameron recommends an exercise to people who are trying to find their creativity. I suggest the same exercise to coachees to help them develop their self-awareness.

Every morning, as soon as she gets up, the coachee should write an A4 page of long-hand. It is just stream-of-consciousness writing – 'oh dear another day at least the sun is shining wish I could stay home. But there's that meeting – what on earth shall I wear – I can hear the motorbike next door, must be eight o'clock...' and so on. The text is for no one else to read, and indeed the writer should not reread it for at least a couple of weeks; if they do, they start to become self-conscious about what they are writing and how they are writing it, and that counteracts the purpose.

The purpose is to bring to consciousness one's preoccupations, and so learn more about what is really driving us, what we really hope for, and what is going on in our inner world.

The coachee may read what she has written over the days or weeks before the next coaching session; or she may just continue the morning pages indefinitely and see what emerges.

One senior executive I worked with, for example, became newly aware through her morning pages of her sense of humour, and her ironic 'take' on everyday events. She realised that she had rather a serious persona at work, and was not actually being herself. She started to bring much more of her dry wit into her work, and enjoyed her working days more, and also discovered people enjoyed working alongside her more.

Telling the truth in the here-and-now

We have already emphasised many times the nature of the coaching relationship, and the beliefs, values and skills of the coach. It is a demanding environment, highly demanding of the coach's integrity and discipline. It has to be, in order to be safe.

Because of its special nature, which the coach works hard to establish, it offers a special opportunity. That is the opportunity for the coach to give feedback to her coachee.

Why is this a special opportunity?

- First, because the coachee can (and probably will) have more confidence that the feedback she receives from the coach is done with one sole purpose: to help the coachee achieve her goals. There is no hidden agenda, and the coach is as sure as a person ever can be that he is giving feedback with totally positive intent.
- Second, the coach has lots of opportunity to experience the coachee's behaviour directly. He experiences her communicating with, and relating to, him; he sees her solving problems and making decisions; he experiences how she organises and keeps appointments; and many other things besides. Not only that, he hears her describe many dif-

ferent situations and people. He has lots of indirect experience of her behaviour too.

- Third, the coach is skilled at giving feedback and helping the coachee interpret it.

This combination of attitude, knowledge and skill is pretty rare. Most of the people who know the coachee really well won't be detached, and solely interested in helping her achieve her goals. Even her nearest and dearest will have things to gain and lose from speaking directly and openly with her about her behaviour.

I remember Richard Boyatzis (personal communication, 2000) telling the story of his much-loved wife asking him for feedback on how she looked in a favourite red dress. She had put on some weight, and in truth it was a bit too tight. But was Richard going to give her that feedback? I leave you to guess!

People who are genuinely detached probably won't have the information – and certainly won't have it in the detail the coach has. And even supposing someone else had the information and the right intent, what are the chances he would have the kind of skills that enable a coach to tell an unwelcome truth without leaving a coachee feeling incompetent, unloved ... or simply confused?

So a coach has a powerful opportunity to develop a coachee's self-awareness in the here-and-now. When she can see something about the coachee's behaviour that could really help him achieve his goals, she can tell it. And when she sees something about his behaviour that might really get in the way, she can tell that too.

Also, simply reflecting back her experience of the coachee can be helpful. What is distinctive about him to the coach? What does she notice? But remember that ultimately there should be a link with the coachee's goals, and that link should be made explicit. For that is the contract between coach and coachee. The coach has no mandate to give feedback about something simply because it has a big effect on her (apart from issues to do with the coaching contract such as keeping to sessions and so on).

For example, I once coached a manager who always answered questions very precisely. I really had to work hard to get the big picture, and often felt I was being 'drip-fed' information. But the coaching agenda was about his work/life balance, and feedback on his communication style would have been at best irrelevant and at worst destructive.

When something happens in the coaching session that illustrates something important and relevant to the coachee's goals outside the session, it can be gold dust. For example, I find coachees often relive incidents as they tell me about them. Their tone of voice and demeanour change and become what they were in the incident itself. I have often given feedback on how that tone of voice and demeanour come across.

One manager I coached had no idea there was contempt in his voice when he was retelling a conversation with his boss. One of his goals was to improve his relationship with his boss! My feedback produced an important development in his self-awareness, and not just in his self-awareness in relation to that specific conversation.

Of course, to take advantage of this powerful opportunity, a coach must have a high level of self-awareness herself (see Chapter 7). Otherwise she can't be sure why she is telling this particular truth at this point. Is she doing it to re-establish her own authority as a coach? Or out of irritation? Or because she wants to appear smart? (Coaches are human too and so not free from these kinds of motives; what they do is work hard to recognise them and not act on them.)

Telling the truth in the here-and-now has to be done carefully. Where the truth is hard for the coachee to hear (see Chapter 11 on 'danger points'), it may temporarily damage rapport. Then the coach needs to re-establish it. Also, in giving feedback, both positive and negative, the coach temporarily takes a position of power relative to her coachee. She will need to restore the coachee to his rightful position 'in charge' of his own development as soon as she can (see the section in Chapter 9 on managing needs in relation to controlling).

Chapter 15

Reflecting

Introduction

When you ask a group of managers which word they are drawn to, 'action' or 'reflection', 75 per cent will choose 'action'. They see 'action' as what they are paid to take, and they are more often than not chosen as managers because of their habit of effective action. They decide, they organise, they direct; they intervene to ensure order and progress. They produce, they deliver, they get results; they make things happen.

As coaches, we are in the business – among other things – of enabling and encouraging reflection. Coaching conversations happen in the pauses between actions. Sometimes these are long pauses, as in a two-hour session between a senior manager and her 'executive coach'. Sometimes they are short pauses, as in a snatched conversation between colleagues on the way to a meeting. But always there is some suspension of action for reflection, some interruption of doing for thinking about doing.

Given most of our clients' natural and instinctive preference for action over reflection, we should spend a little time explaining why we coaches set so much store by the latter. Is it just because reflection is what comes naturally to us coaches? Perhaps we are generally thinkers rather than doers, peddling our preference to the doers of this world. Or is it rather because reflection is a necessary balance to action, and without it none of us will realise our potential?

Let me describe some of the ways in which reflection informs us and enhances our ability to get the outcomes we want.

When we reflect, we access more of our own resources. If we rush straight into action, we shall tend to do the first thing that comes into our head, to respond instinctively. When we reflect, we have the possibility of remembering differ-

Given most of our clients' natural and instinctive preference for action over reflection, we should spend a little time explaining why we coaches set so much store by the latter.

ent approaches we have used in the past, of reminding ourselves of what we know about the situation that is relevant, and of mustering all our knowledge and skill to do the best we can.

Here is an example of this working in practice. A senior manager I worked with was asked to give a presentation to three hundred people. There was a standard format for such events in the bank she worked for, and she was preparing to follow it. In one of our coaching sessions, she reflected on how good she is at establishing an informal environment, at using images from music and film (great passions of hers) to illustrate points, and at chatting with people rather than lecturing. She decided to run the presentation very differently from the customary format, and the style she has introduced has set new standards in her organisation.

You will no doubt readily call to mind many situations where your first impulse would have led you to a much less effective use of your strengths than your second – or tenth! – impulse after reflection.

A related point is that when we reflect we are more likely afterwards to act creatively. Quick action tends to follow established programmes. The senior manager I referred to just now had temporarily 'forgotten about' her vast knowledge of music and films. It belonged to a part of her life that was separate from work. She needed a little time to see that expertise from somewhere else could be brought to bear on her work challenge.

A further related point is that when we reflect we end up with more choices. At first it might seem 'there is only one thing to do'; as we reflect, we realise that there are many things we could do. Or we often polarise our choice on first encountering a problem or opportunity. We think in terms of 'either/or': 'Either he has to go, or I do.' 'Either I get promotion this year, or I leave.' On reflection, we become aware of more complex sets of possibilities.

Reflection enables us to see the interconnectedness of things. We are less likely after reflecting to suffer from 'unintended consequences' of our actions. We are more likely to identify the points of leverage, the actions that will yield the best return for least effort. It takes time to explore and understand the nature of the social and organisational systems around us. Reflection gives us that time.

In a reflective state of mind, we become more aware of our feelings and of what our feelings are trying to tell us. Many coaching sessions I have given have centred on the client feeling her anger at some organisational 'injustice', exploring exactly what she is angry about, and deciding what to do about it.

In a reflective state of mind, we become more able to look at situations from other people's points of view. We can plan actions that are more likely to resolve a conflict, or establish a good definition of interfacing roles for us and a colleague, or get a new working relationship off to a good start, as a result of taking time to imagine what things look and feel like from the other person's point of view.

I was working with a management consultant on some difficulties he had with a particular colleague. We were imagining together how she saw him. Suddenly he realised how intimidating he seemed to her. At that point, he made a decision to act to reduce that impression of intimidation. (Up to that point, he had hidden from this difficult relationship by being distant and hence more intimidating.) Little by little, the relationship began to improve.

Having reflected on the positive effects of reflection, let us now turn our attention to what reflection really is. Only then can we be clear about how to encourage it.

Reflection is not the same as thought. There are many kinds of thought, of which reflection is just one. There are very destructive and limiting kinds of thought, for example. Obsessive thinking would be one extreme example, where we find ourselves thinking over and over again about the same thing in a way that feeds our anxiety.

Many of us who have been in troublesome relationships with our boss will recognise that kind of thinking. We brood over all the slights we have suffered that day at the hand of our boss, we relive moments of humiliation and rage, and we become increasingly despairing. That kind of thinking is not reflection.

There is the kind of thinking that at its extreme is called 'mania'. That is thinking centred on fantasies about how clever, successful and good we are. Just like obsessive thinking, mania feeds itself; it does not explore reality but creates an artificial alternative to reality. It can be fun, but it is not reflection.

Then there is the kind of thinking we might call 'procrastination'. It may involve oscillating between planning two diametrically opposed courses of action. As soon as plans for one course have been advanced, we change our minds and start planning the other. We are thinking in order to avoid taking action. That is not reflection.

It is important to distinguish between these different kinds of thinking. Managers are rightly suspicious of thinking that replaces action, of thinking that allows things to remain exactly as they are, and quite simply wastes time.

But reflection should save time. It is thinking directed at understanding all aspects of reality more fully, and at planning action that we shall commit to and stands the best chance of achieving our goals. It is characterised by openness and creativity: new perspectives and new information are welcomed and spontaneously generated. It is also characterised by calmness, by absence of anxiety.

Imagine a woman sitting comfortably in a chair, her chin resting lightly on her hand, her expression tranquil, her gaze slightly unfocused and directed to the distance. She is a picture of ready and relaxed openness. She is accessing her inner world, without losing awareness of her external world. She is reflecting.

> Managers are rightly suspicious of thinking that replaces action, of thinking that allows things to remain exactly as they are, and quite simply wastes time.

How can this kind of thinking be encouraged?

Pitch, tone and pace of voice

I hesitated about putting material about pace, tone and pitch of voice in a section on technique, because it is hard to change these characteristics of yourself and easy, if you try, to come across as insincere or stilted. But it is such an important aspect of encouraging a reflective state of mind I feel it cannot be omitted.

The way we speak has more impact on whether a person will respond with action or reflection than anything we might actually say. And it is in fact possible to develop the right speaking voice, if we work 'from the inside out' (that is, if we focus on getting our inner state right and let our outer behaviours follow naturally from that).

The pitch, tone and pace of voice need to be those that convey calm. In general, that means a low pitch, a melodic tone and a slow pace. To understand this point, imagine the opposite for a moment. You need someone to take action, and to take action fast.

You are a passenger in their car. They need to stop. They are about to hit the car in front. You raise your voice, and bark out 'You're going to hit that guy – stop!' as fast as you can. With any luck, you will bypass your driver's conscious mind completely and his foot will jam down on the brake pedal. Then he may well turn to you and say 'What the…!?' Now you can have a reflective conversation if you choose.

So if we are naturally blessed with a low, melodic voice, and a measured tempo of speaking, we have some built-in advantages when it comes to encouraging reflection.

But if we need to develop the ability to speak in that way, we can do it through ourselves learning how to relax and reflect. Then the voice will tend to follow, as a natural consequence of the change in our thought processes.

We need to get rid of any impatience, any sense of pressure; so it is important not to embark on a piece of reflecting towards the end of a coaching session when time is running out. It is also important that we arrive at a coaching session rested and relaxed. During the session we should work hard to eliminate impatient or tense thoughts from our minds. If we start to think 'My coachee really ought to do this' or 'It's time we got some movement on that,' our voice will betray that we want action not reflection, and that is what we are likely to encourage.

When we feel curious (see Chapter 6, the section on 'Questioning'), our voice is more likely to become lower, more melodic and slower. And smiling will take it in that direction too. So look for things to appreciate and things that intrigue you, and you are more likely to speak in a way that encourages reflection.

'Differentiating questions'

There is a particular form of question that encourages reflection, simply because it cannot be answered without a search through one's memory and some inner mental processing. It is a question that asks someone to differentiate, to compare and contrast, and come up with a conclusion. Examples are these:

- What is the most difficult aspect of your role?
- When are you least stressed by that?
- Who is the best example of that?
- What is the strongest reason for change?

And so on. It is the differentiating words such as 'most', 'least', 'best', 'strongest' that promote reflection, and questions such as these are unlikely to be answered immediately. The pause that occurs as people think about the answer slows the pace of conversation, and again encourages a more reflective approach. Often that mood of reflection will continue after the specific question has been answered.

'Model' a reflective state of mind

We have already described how reflecting yourself as a coach can lead to a change in way of speaking that helps a coachee reflect. It can also influence the coachee through that powerful form of social learning, 'modelling', which we first mentioned in Chapter 4 where we were exploring how a 'desire to learn' can spread from coach to coachee.

It can be particularly powerful for the coach to reflect between sessions on things that have been said, and to talk with the coachee about those reflections and what has come out of them.

An example of this occurred recently for me when I had had what seemed to me a rather unfocused and low-energy session with a coachee of mine. I began the next session by talking about how I had reflected on whether the last session had been useful to him, and decided to revisit with him the goals we had agreed for the coaching process. He in turn became very thoughtful about his own motivations for change; he had 'caught' a reflective state of mind from me.

Of course, with active listening and questioning we are modelling reflection all the time, and this is one of the most valuable things we do as coaches. As Kets de Vries, Insead professor and leadership guru, has written (1984):

'To create effective organisations, an effort must be made to help executives admit their emotions and practise their capacity for self-observation. The tendency of many executives to fly into action without the balance of reflection has to be carefully monitored.'

Chapter 16

Mapping systems

Introduction

When we are under pressure, and often when we are on our own, we think linearly. We understand what's going on in terms of a single cause and effect. 'He rubbished my idea, so I felt angry.' 'We missed the deadline, so the client gave the next piece of work to someone else.' 'My boss doesn't keep me in the picture, so I don't tell him what I'm up to either.'

It is in our nature to try to find meaning and reasons in what happens to us, and the simplest way of doing this, and the way which comes most naturally to us, is to do it in terms of linear cause and effect.

There are two problems with this way of thinking. The first is that it simply doesn't accurately reflect reality. In life, pretty much everything is pretty much connected to everything else. (That is slightly overstating it, but you get the point.) So if we want to understand any situation or relationship fully, linear thinking won't get us there.

The second problem is that if you are looking for ways of changing things (and that is often what we are doing in coaching), then focusing on single causes limits your problem-solving. You need to think about the whole picture to have the best chance of finding a good leverage point for change.

What we need help in doing is in thinking not linearly, but 'systemically'. Peter Senge, Director of the Center for Organizational Learning at MIT's Sloan School of Management, has done more than anyone to clarify and popularise the idea of 'systems thinking', and its importance for healthy organisational life. His book *The Fifth Discipline Fieldbook* (1994) is a good source of information. What I want to do here is describe a few tools a coach can use to help her coachee gain a broad understanding of the whole context of an issue he has, and so think 'systemically'.

Diagrams and doodles

When we look at pictures, our right brain is more active, and that is the side that we need more from to think systemically. So it is a good idea for there to be paper and pencils always to hand in a coaching session. Whatever coach and coachee draw to represent what's going on will help, but here are some types of drawing that I use all the time.

Maps of all the people a coachee has relationships with at work, and how they relate to each other and other significant 'stakeholders' are useful. A drawing helps patterns emerge; a manager and I were looking at her 'stakeholder map' the other day, and it suddenly dawned on her that all the problematic relationships were with people who had worked at one time or another for a peer of hers who had not supported her promotion to a board-level appointment.

These stakeholder maps are also useful reference points over a series of coaching sessions; they help a coachee chart his progress at networking, and at building the whole web of relationships that he needs to be successful. Sometimes I will ask a coachee to 'score' the health of each key relationship on the map, and keep track of this score and how it changes over time.

Timelines are useful too. These look linear, but they help people see connections over time, and where key events are. They help people recognise that many issues have a long history, and that the key to their resolution may lie in something that happened before they were personally involved.

A senior lawyer I worked with who was having a short series of coaching sessions following her return from maternity leave found it helpful to chart a whole series of events leading to a current serious client problem. She drew a timeline marking key events for this client from before her maternity leave through her absence and right up to the present time. The timeline helped her identify exactly what had upset her client – not the handover as such, as she had originally thought, but a confusion over two people's roles and responsibilities following that handover.

Sometimes it's helpful to a coachee to categorise events on a timeline in some way. For example, the line may dip when the coachee remembers it was a 'low point' and peak when it was a 'high point'. This kind of categorisation enables coach and coachee to see patterns and trends – such as all the 'low points' being recent!

'Mind maps' can be useful too. Tony Buzan invented the technique of 'mind-mapping' in the 1970s (see Buzan and Buzan 1993). Instead of noting down all your thinking on a subject in a list (which encourages left-brain and linear thinking only), you put the focus of your thinking in the centre of a page and jot down all the thoughts and ideas that seem connected, linking them with the main focus and each other with lines in an ever-expanding spider's web. An example of a mind-map is shown in Figure 2. Mind maps encourage us to think laterally as well as analytically, and so they help with systems thinking.

Apart from these fairly structured diagrams, all sorts of doodles and jottings can be helpful. Draw smiley and miserable faces to represent successes and disappointments, columns of pros and cons, circles with

Figure 2   *'Mind mapping' – a way of following a natural train of thought.*

segments to represent proportions of time, a two-by-two matrix with a personal SWOT analysis – and don't worry if your drawings are childish and your lines wobbly!

And of course it's best of all when the coachee picks up the pencil and starts drawing. The key thing is to help people think visually, which leads naturally into a greater tendency to think systemically.

'Force field analysis'

Of all the tools to help with systems thinking, this is in my view the best. It is simple, and powerful. It is fun to do, and it is best done by more than one person working together. So it is ideal for coaching.

An example of a completed force field analysis is shown in Figure 3 (overleaf). I have chosen a personal rather than a work-related goal, just to indicate how widely applicable this tool is. I have known people use it to help them move house successfully, change job, learn a new skill – there really is no goal that it doesn't help with.

The first step is to articulate the goal (see Chapter 13). Then coach and coachee brainstorm together, and list, all the 'driving forces'. These are forces in the coachee's life that move her in the right direction, in the direction of her goal. They may be feelings, events, other people, facts about the situation, and so on. When the coachee feels the picture of driving forces is reasonably complete, coach and coachee move on to brainstorm all the 'resisting forces'. These are everything in the coachee's life preventing her achieving her goal.

The next step is to draw arrows representing the strength of each force at the moment. The longer the arrow, the stronger the force. So, in the example, the coachee is looking in the mirror often, and feeling very bad when she does: that is a very strong driving force. She doesn't much like her old summer clothes, so the fact that they don't fit her is only a weak driving force: she isn't much influenced by it at the moment. On the resisting force side, there are three very strong forces really preventing her moving towards her goal.

Once the picture is complete, coach and coachee can step back and see what it tells them. Sometimes it suggests the goal is unachievable at the moment: the driving forces are too few and the resisting forces too many. But more often it will show leverage points: weak driving forces, which can be increased, and strong resisting forces, which can be

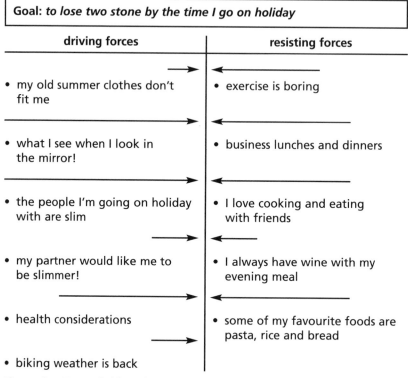

Figure 3 *'Force field analysis' – a technique for understanding the context of change*

reduced or eliminated. Actions that achieve this will make a major contribution to the coachee achieving her goal.

In the example, she might decide to buy herself some new summer clothes she really likes in the size she is trying to reach; that will increase the strength of this driving force and may tip the balance. Or she may make a pact with her closest friends that when they eat together they will eat low-calorie foods; then it may be that she turns the strong resisting force into a driving force, as her friends start to encourage and support her diet.

By providing an overview of the system of driving and resisting forces that are holding constant a particular state of affairs, force field analysis enables effective planning to achieve goals. It also represents a straightforward way to encourage 'systems thinking'.

'Commitment charting'

In the vast majority of goals that people have, other people are involved. And it will often be their actions, in support of or in resistance to our goals, which will determine how successful we shall be at achieving them. 'Commitment charting' is a tool a coach can use to help his coachee explore, understand and respond effectively to the system of positive and negative influences represented by other people's commitment to or against her goal.

An empty commitment chart is shown in Figure 4. The first thing coach and coachee need to do is put down the names of everyone who will be affected by the change the coachee wants to make. That is often an interesting exercise in itself, particularly if the coach encourages his coachee to think broadly and laterally about this. 'No man is an island', and no change affects only one person. Commitment charting enables a picture to be seen of the ripples that spread into a person's 'community' from the pebble of her change.

Then an X is put on the chart to indicate the current attitude of each person listed to the coachee's desired change. Sometimes the coachee doesn't know, and then she may realise she needs to find out.

Now an O is put on the chart to indicate the attitude each person needs to have in order for the change to be achieved. Can they continue in ignorance, because they have no influence? Or do they need to take the lead in promoting the change, because they have a huge amount of influence?

These are thought-provoking conversations for the coachee, and can result in further insight into her own attitude to the change, and to revision of her goals.

I did a commitment chart with a manager who was trying to introduce an IT-based client management system into the consultancy he worked for. After he'd done the chart, very objectively and thoroughly, he looked at it and said: 'It's absolutely clear this organisation isn't ready for a system like this. I'm pushing water uphill. I'm going to put my energies elsewhere.' Seeing the whole social system he was working with enabled him to understand more fully than he had before exactly what he was up against.

Finally, the completed chart shows where changes in attitude are needed. Planning to achieve those changes can begin.

Change objective:					

People affected by the change	Attitude to the change				
	unaware	resistant	neutral	supportive	leading

X = where they are
O = where they need to be

Figure 4   *'Commitment charting' – a technique for exploring and understanding resistance to change*

The 'why' question

The last tool for encouraging and enabling systems thinking is the simplest of all, and the best. It is the question 'why?' The power in this question comes when it is used not just once (this encourages linear, cause-and-effect thinking) but repeatedly. In fact, the Japanese have a continuous improvement technique they call 'the five why's', which forces people to look at a huge slice of the organisational system before they start to plan to solve a problem.

I don't recommend the formal 'five why's' technique for the coaching context; it is too cumbersome. But if a

The last tool for encouraging and enabling systems thinking is the simplest of all, and the best. It is the question 'why?'

coach asks 'why' repeatedly it can lead to a deeper and truer under-standing of a problem, and to a better basis for solving that problem. Clearly, asking 'why' like a parrot or a small child would be irritating to any coachee. The technique is to remember always to help the coachee explore further. After all, if the problem were simple, she wouldn't have brought it to her coach; she would have just got on and solved it.

Here is a small extract from a coaching dialogue that made good use of the 'why' question.

> Coachee: 'I've lost trust in my sales manager. We used to work so well together, and now I feel I can't trust him.'
>
> Coach: 'Now why's that?'
>
> Coachee: 'He's been bad-mouthing a decision of mine to the rest of the staff.'
>
> Coach: 'Have you any idea why he should do that, when you had such a good relationship before?'
>
> Coachee: 'I guess he's pretty sensitive at the moment, and I didn't have time to consult him about the decision first.'
>
> Coach: 'So why's he sensitive at the moment?'
>
> And so on.

The dialogue is shortened and simplified, but hopefully you can see how repeated use of the question 'why' extends the frame of reference, and hence the coachee's understanding of what's going on, bit by bit. Eventually she will feel she has got to 'the heart of the matter' and that will be useful to her.

Chapter 17

Exploring and understanding other people's positions

Introduction

The commonest type of issue people bring to workplace coaching is a problem with an important work relationship. There are a couple of reasons for this. First, people do cause each other problems, all the time, at work. Organisations are social systems. The hopes and fears each of us has in relation to our place in the 'tribe' and our position in society are evoked by organisational life. Do we really belong? How far up the 'pecking order' are we? Do we like and can we trust our colleagues?

Also, the organisation we work in evokes memories and patterns established in the 'organisation' we started our lives in: our family. We feel jealous of our siblings (colleagues). We compete for our parents' (bosses') attention. We become dependent on our family's (company's) approval, and then we find it constricting and think about leaving home (our job).

The nature of organisational life often makes it hard for people to treat each other compassionately and consistently. As Peter Frost discovered in the research that underpins his book *Toxic Emotions at Work* (2003):

'If you're not contributing to the bottom line, you'll be disposed of. This is true despite the company's assertions that "we are about people". Organisations have to make their first priority their own survival, and that often results in damage to individuals and damage to relationships.'

The second reason why problems with work relationships become a focus for coaching is that the confidential coaching relationship is often the only context in which it feels safe to a coachee to talk about such problems. The risks of the person he has the problem with finding out he had discussed it could be huge. It could turn a problematic relationship into a disastrous one. It could damage either or both parties' careers.

Finally, a coach may be the one person a coachee can trust not to judge her negatively and 'side' with the other person. The nature of the coaching relationship, as we have described in the first three parts of this book, gives the coachee that confidence.

When these problems are brought to coaching, the coach has many ways in which she might be helpful. These range, for example, from listening and allowing her coachee to express what may be quite painful feelings, to helping him plan a course of action to improve the relationship. But one of the most valuable things a coach can do is help the coachee, when it is appropriate, put himself in 'the other person's shoes'. The insights he will have, if he does this effectively, will enormously increase both his understanding of what is going on and his resourcefulness in thinking about what to do about it.

Let us look at some tools and some techniques the coach can use to put a coachee in another person's shoes.

> One of the most valuable things a coach can do is help the coachee, when it is appropriate, put himself in 'the other person's shoes'.

The 'what would they say' question

A coach can bring the other person in a problematic relationship 'into the room' by simply asking his coachee: 'What would he/she say if they were here now?' Useful times to ask this question are just after your coachee has finished describing the problem from her point of view, or when she is considering a particular course of action. In the second case, the focus of the question needs to change slightly to: 'How will they respond to this?'

You can help your coachee actually get inside the other person by painting a picture before asking the question. You might do it like this: 'Imagine x were sitting just there, and had been listening to our conversation. What would they say about it all?' If your coachee gives a quick answer to the question, it probably hasn't resulted in any extra insight. But if she pauses and appears to be thinking, and then answers the question thoughtfully, she may well be succeeding in making the leap of empathy and truly seeing things from her colleague's point of view.

Meta-mirror

Meta-mirror is a well-known technique in neuro-linguistic programming, which can be much more effective than the simple 'what would they say' question. It works because its structure elicits right-brain as well as left-brain involvement. It can feel rather strange to coachees, though, so it has to be introduced carefully, with plenty of explanation on why it might be helpful. Sometimes coachees will still dismiss it as an artificial exercise, and then of course it is best left.

In meta-mirror, the coach sets up three positions, often with three chairs. One chair represents the coachee (it will probably be the chair the coachee is currently sitting in). The second chair represents the other person in the problematic relationship. The third chair represents a detached and neutral observer.

First the coachee is asked to describe the problem from her own position. She is asked to imagine the other person sitting in the second chair – she may want to arrange the chairs so their relative positions are typical of how she and the other person sit together. (I have had coachees who point out the other person never sits in their presence, for example; then we take the second chair away.) What does she see, think and feel as she sits opposite the other person? The more specifically she can describe her perceptions, thoughts and feelings, the better meta-mirror will work.

When the coachee has said all she wants to from her own position, the coach invites her to move to the second position. She should move physically; the physical movement elicits more ability to imagine what things look like from the other person's point of view. The coach should, for the same reason, encourage the coachee to sit as the other person would, to do anything which helps her to 'become' that other person for a few moments.

The coach then says something along the lines of: '(Coachee's name) is still sitting in that chair. Now you are x and you are looking at (coachee's name). What do you see, think and feel as you look at her?' The coach should help his coachee imagine, by asking more specific questions such as: 'Is there any tension for you anywhere? What is it about (coachee's name) that you are seeing which makes you feel tense? What are you thinking about that?' and so on.

Some people can make very effective use of this opportunity to stand in another person's shoes, and they will start talking about 'I' and 'me' as if they were indeed that other person. Others find it hard or awkward to make the leap, so clearly the coach has to adapt accordingly how long and how specifically she works with them in this position.

Finally, the coach invites the coachee to move to the 'observer' position. She is asked to imagine the coachee and the other person are still in their positions: what does this detached observer, from a sort of god-like perspective, notice about them? What thoughts and feelings does she have? The coach is still asking questions to prompt and encourage, but not offering any views of his own.

The very last step is for the coachee to return to her own position and reflect on what she learned. Are there things she will do differently in consequence? Sometimes a coachee will want to repeat the meta-mirror and will find she can use it to test out the effects of different approaches to the relationship.

Full role play

One step further than meta-mirror is a full role play. This is useful when a coachee wants to try out an approach, perhaps rehearse a conversation, and get as much understanding as possible about how it will affect the relationship. The coach and coachee work out what approach is going to be taken, and the coachee plays the part of the other person.

(The coach should never take the part of the 'other person'; the coachee's feelings of distrust may transfer from that other person to the coach and damage her relationship with her coach.) The coach tries the approach, and the coachee discovers what it feels like.

Again, this technique is most powerful when the coachee is able and willing to 'become' the other person. Then she can get an enormous amount of information very fast about how that other person will respond.

How is it that these techniques work? They are making use of the fact that we have a lot more information about another person than we normally consciously access and use. Particularly when we find a relationship difficult or stressful, we suppress a lot of the information we have and defend ourselves by focusing mostly on our own position.

The techniques of meta-mirror and role play have the potential to get round our defences, and bring to our conscious minds all those things that we know about the other person but have been ignoring. They can do this precisely because they are not the 'normal' way we relate to others, but because they are not normal, many people are uncomfortable using them. All a coach can do is describe the technique and its benefits, and then let his coachee decide whether to use it.

Even when these techniques are not appropriate in their full form, the coach can incorporate elements from them in a perfectly natural way. One example of this is the 'what would they say' question we looked at earlier. Another is when the coach summarises something the coachee is considering saying to the other person and asks 'so how do you think they will respond?'

> The techniques of meta-mirror and role play have the potential to get round our defences, and bring to our conscious minds all those things that we know about the other person but have been ignoring.

All these methods are ways of eliciting empathy, the capacity of one human being to imagine what another is feeling.

Chapter 18

Creative problem-solving

Introduction

If a coach is to increase the range of choice open to a coachee (and that is an important part of enabling her to achieve her goals), then new ideas need to be had – by coach, by coachee, and by both. People often come to coaching when they feel 'stuck'; they've tried all the obvious things to make progress, and none of them has worked. They need something new.

Several of the coaches I know and work with find this requirement for creativity daunting. They worry that they are themselves 'not particularly creative people', so how will they be able to help their coachees here?

There are a couple of things to say about this. The first is that it amazes me that the issue of 'creativity' is such a difficult one for so many of us. There is no human being on the planet who isn't creative. It is in our nature to make new things, either literally or metaphorically. That is why we have such an enormous cerebral cortex (in comparison with other species).

We shouldn't be intimidated and downcast by the fact we can't compare our creative achievements with those of a Picasso or a Mozart. We should look at these examples of exceptional creativity and remind ourselves that we have that part of humanity too, although not to such a degree. We show it in making jokes, in finding an answer to puzzles, in playing with our children – the examples are too numerous to list. And we certainly are creative enough to give our coachees what they need.

The second point is that, whatever a coachee might say they want, they are unlikely to benefit from heaps of creativity from their coach about their issues. In fact, if the coach has lots of fantastic ideas readily springing to mind about a problem the coachee has wrestled with for months, how will that make the coachee feel? Certainly not more confident (see

Chapter 2, and the dangers of giving a coachee 'the answer'). What the coachee needs most is access to her own creativity, and the coach is there to help her get it.

There are some aspects of technique that are particularly useful here.

Providing safety and humour

In Parts One and Two we talked about how essential it is for the coachee to feel 'safe' in the coaching environment. We pointed out several reasons for this, but we didn't mention explicitly the important relationship between safety and creativity.

To be creative, we need to feel free from threat. Fear drives out creativity – at a physiological level blood carries oxygen away from our brain and towards the muscles that we will need to fight or flee; we are unlikely to have our best ideas when our brains are depleted. Also, fear tends to narrow (and sharpen) our focus, a good thing for action, but a barrier to lateral

> To be creative, we need to feel free from threat. Fear drives out creativity

thinking. And we simply don't feel like being creative when we are anxious; we feel like closing down and defending ourselves, rather than opening our eyes and minds to new possibilities.

So by making it part of her business to provide a 'safe' environment in all the ways we have described so far in this book, a coach is already doing something that is likely to increase significantly her coachee's creativity.

Humour is often a sign of safety and relaxation. In fact, we often comment on how people will laugh and make jokes to 'release tension'. We talked in Chapter 7 about the value of 'a habit of seeing the funny side if things' in a coach, providing she is laughing with and not at her coachee! Playfulness promotes creative thinking.

A colleague of mine was working with a coachee who wanted to develop more 'emotional intelligence'. They were laughing together about examples of their own 'emotional stupidity' when his coachee came up with the idea of giving himself an 'EQ' rating on his own behaviour at the end of every meeting he attended. It turned out to be one of the best pieces of development he did, increasing his self-awareness and understanding of his own 'emotional footprint' and enabling him to make some changes in how he prepared for and dealt with difficult encounters.

'Linking' questions

It is often said that we only use a fraction of the resources available to us. This is true on so many levels. It is true at a neurological level: we have much more processing capacity in our brains than we ever use. It is true at a social level: we miss opportunities all the time to get help, advice, or support from people who would gladly give it if they only knew we needed it. And it is true on a psychological level: we seem to categorise our abilities according to which part of our life they seem most relevant to, and neglect to use them in other parts of our lives.

Coaching can enable people to make links between a work problem they need to solve and another area of their lives where they solve problems like that one easily. What the coachee then experiences is a flow of 'new ideas', as knowledge and skill move from one 'psychological domain' to another. It is 'linking questions' that enable this to happen.

Linking questions are questions like these:

- When have you solved a problem like this before? What happened?
- Where else in your life do you deal with anything like this? How do you deal with it?
- Have you ever been in a situation like this before? Tell the story.
- Do you know anyone else like this? How do you handle them?

You may remember the coachee of mine who found a way to give an excellent business presentation by drawing on the skills she was known for in her personal and social life (Chapter 15). I had asked her the linking question 'What do your friends enjoy about talking with you?' and that had produced a whole new line of thinking for her.

I also often ask people to talk about how they coach and develop their children – the natural parenting skills many of us use every day can give us insight into how best to encourage learning in others at work. One senior executive I worked with experienced a personal revelation about why his management style might not be working as well as he would like when he reflected on how he gets (and fails to get) co-operation from his teenage children!

The more we can remember as coaches that there is far more to our coachees' lives and abilities than their job title and role, the more we shall ask them the questions that enable them to access all their own resources of knowledge, wit, wisdom and skill.

Of course, the greatest linking questions of all are the ones that prompt a coachee to link his experience of someone else with his own

The more we can remember as coaches that there is far more to our coachees' lives and abilities than their job title and role, the more we shall ask them the questions that enable them to access all their own resources of knowledge, wit, wisdom and skill.

experience. In the last chapter we explored how a coach can help a coachee 'put herself in someone else's shoes' in order to find new solutions to old relationship problems. We were making use of the fact that we all carry around with us the greatest resource available for understanding another person: our shared humanity with that other person.

We can help our coachees access that resource by asking questions such as:

- How would you want to be given that information?
- What would you be feeling now, if you were her?
- Have you ever behaved the way he is? What was going on then?

Stupidity

I am probably overstating this technique with the rather provocative choice of title, but I do think that when we as coaches stop trying to be very smart and allow ourselves to offer crazy or even stupid ideas, that can liberate creativity in our coachees. For one thing, it communicates the message through deeds as well as words that trying new things, even at the risk of a mistake or a failure, is healthy. For another, a 'bad' idea can lead to someone else having a good one. In seeing how an idea just will not work, a coachee becomes clearer about what might work instead.

I suggested recently to an overloaded partner in an accounting firm that he should have two secretaries. He knew that was a crazy idea, and actually I didn't think it would work myself. But I was at my wit's end trying to help him get his workload under control, particularly since he had a secretary to whom he was devoted but who wasn't up to the job.

My crazy idea led him to reflect on the fact that the senior partner had an 'executive assistant' – a young accountant with high potential, seconded to the partner's office for a year to act as PA but also learn more about the politics and strategy of the firm. My coachee ended up recruiting an executive assistant for himself, something that had never occurred to him before.

In some ways, we aren't drawing fully on our own resources as coaches if we don't come up with 'crazy ideas'. For after all, we typically have very different backgrounds, experiences and motivations from those we coach. So ideas that seem good to us will often be unworkable in practice; but that doesn't mean we shouldn't offer them. Of course, we must do so in a way that doesn't damage our 'credibility' (see Chapter 8), but that's easily done.

We can acknowledge that we move in a different world and see things from a very different perspective, and that sometimes this means we offer ideas to our coachees that they know cannot work in their world. Our willingness to take risks – the risk of looking stupid, the risk of being wrong – will create an environment in which our coachees are more willing to take risks. That is the essence of creativity.

Chapter 19

Monitoring progress

Introduction

As an intermediate skier always keen to improve, I have benefited hugely from Timothy Gallwey and Robert Kriegel's book, *Inner Skiing* (1997). The approach they advocate stems from the central idea (somewhat revolutionary in sports coaching) that people learn best not by being given sets of instructions but by being encouraged to tap into their own 'natural learning process'.

A key part of that process is building awareness of what your body is actually doing, rather than filling your head with thoughts of what it should be doing. Improvement often occurs then with no 'instruction' from the coach. Instead, the learner develops expertise in knowing what he does that brings him closer to what he wants, and what he does that takes him further away. He then does more of the former, and less of the latter, and hey presto! He gets what he wants.

The relevance to coaching generally is obvious. Coaches should be helping coachees to monitor their progress towards their goals not only because that will build their commitment to those goals, but also because the very act of measuring progress means they are more likely to make some.

The 1–10 scale

If you ask someone to increase their awareness of some aspect of their behaviour, they can be a little lost as to how to do it. They need some practical way of doing it to focus on. The 1–10 scale provides it.

Here is an example of the 1–10 scale in action. I have a coachee who becomes obviously aggressive, and much less effective, when he feels under threat. He wants to develop his ability to stay cool when others are attacking him unfairly. I have suggested he use the 1–10 scale to monitor his level of 'coolness'. '10' represents his target level of coolness – perfectly calm and able to think clearly and productively about what's going on and what he needs to do. '1' represents the worst it gets – absolutely hot-headed and in the grip of his emotions.

He did this for a couple of weeks, rating himself in the key meetings at various points, and gradually developing an awareness of his emotional 'temperature'.

Two things happened in consequence. First, the simple act of monitoring led to a decrease in hot-headedness. Second, he noticed something that interested him: he got his worst scores when he felt badly prepared for a meeting. He decided to monitor his level of preparedness in the same way. That too improved, and his level of calm continues to improve.

I often use the 1–10 scale to measure progress against the goals of coaching (this is another technique borrowed from brief solution-focused therapy).

A manager had as one of his goals that he needed to improve his relationships with his key stakeholders. We drew up a map of the key relationships (see Chapter 16 for how to do this) and he gave the 'health' of each relationship a score between 1 and 10, where 1 was as bad as it gets, and 10 was his goal. Each session he re-examined the scores to see where he was making progress and where the priorities still were.

There are very few goals the 1–10 rating scale can't be used with. It puts a boundary round what the coachee is trying to achieve, and forces an answer to the question 'are things improving?' It also stops coach and coachee 'fudging' the issue of whether progress is being made. The simplicity and clarity of numbers make them useful.

Sometimes a coachee shows reluctance to use the scale. That can be because I haven't explained the purpose well enough, and it sounds 'gimmicky'. But it can be a sign that he isn't really committed to a particular change. Then it is important to move back into goal-setting (see Chapter 13), because perhaps that change isn't the essence of what he wants to achieve after all. In that case, the 1–10 scale has served another useful purpose, that of clarifying what a coachee truly wants.

Chapter 20

Building commitment to, and capability for, change

Introduction

Most coachees come to coaching because they want something to change. (I have had the occasional coachee who has begun by saying he is simply interested in finding out more about himself, but even with a start like that, an agenda for change usually emerges.)

When it comes to making a change, we are so often our own worst enemies. We really want to, we really mean to, but somehow we sabotage ourselves. We are left unhappy that nothing has changed and also dimly aware that we have no one to blame but ourselves.

So anything a coach can do to help us commit to and be capable of change will be invaluable. So long as she has helped us articulate what we really want, and understand ourselves fully, and come up with ideas for change that will actually take us in the right direction (all work we have explored in the previous chapters of this Part Four), we shall welcome her helping us to bring the changes about. We know we have all kinds of inner barriers to our own desired changes; can she help us remove them?

Here are some tools and some techniques aimed at helping in just that way.

Visualisation

Visualisation is a technique used a great deal in sports coaching and has been found to produce impressive effects.

For example, a psychologist and expert in leadership who was working with the England rugby team (this was before Sir Clive

Woodward's time there) described what he believed to be the most significant coaching intervention he made before a critical away match.

He and the other coaches compiled a video of the team's best moments in recent matches, essentially a video of them winning. It was set to music (music helps people engage in effective visualisation because it stimulates our creative and imaginative right brains), and the team watched it just before going out to play. It produced in each of them a strong picture of themselves as winners, playing at their best – and of course they went on to play at their best in reality and to win.

There are innumerable examples from sport and business of people performing more effectively after they have visualised themselves doing so.

I have, for just one example, a coachee who wanted to improve her presentation skills. We spent a coaching session visualising in detail her giving an excellent presentation. The positive effects were immediate and remarkable, and she still uses visualisation herself just before an important presentation.

The reasons why visualisation works in this way are probably complex. There is of course the element of 'mental rehearsal', which primes our tendency to behave in a particular way. (That's why dwelling on what might go wrong is so counterproductive; it actually makes it more likely that we shall do exactly what we are afraid of doing.) If we imagine ourselves speaking clearly and fluently on a topic, for example, we are rehearsing our performance as we imagine it.

Then visualisation involves relaxation. A coach will enable her coachee to get into a relaxed frame of mind before and during visualisation (it is hard to visualise if you are tense), and the activity of visualisation itself has positive physiological effects: deeper breathing, slower heart rate, and so on. When we are less tense, we are more resourceful.

> There are innumerable examples from sport and business of people performing more effectively after they have visualised themselves doing so.

But the particular point I want to make here about visualisation is that it increases a coachee's commitment to the goal. First, she makes the effort of visualising it. So she invests in her own goal. Second, she increases her self-belief that she can get there. Third, she focuses absolutely on her goal, and drives distractions from her mind. As she does all this, her goal becomes both more believable to her, and more important.

The basic approach to visualisation in a coaching context is as follows.

Ensure through all the other elements of the coaching relationship and work that visualisation is appropriate for this coachee at this time on this issue. The coach needs, for example, to have a good understanding of her particular coachee's propensity for visualisation.

I have a colleague who says he has no ability to see things in his mind at all; when he closes his eyes, everything simply goes black. What he does have is a rich and powerful auditory imagination: he can hear whole scenarios in his mind, and that is how he 'visualises'. The coach also needs to be sure that the outcome the coachee is going to visualise is really one she wants. Visualisation is hard work.

Help your coachee to be relaxed. Again, how you do this will vary for different coachees. It helps if people close their eyes, but that can make some coachees anxious. Suggesting people breathe slowly and deeply, and count to control the speed of their breathing, is also helpful.

Then, in a relaxed and relaxing tone of voice encourage your coachee to visualise a scene as he would like it to be. You may help him with some description of your own – for example, 'the people listening to you are attentive and quiet' – but be careful; you have to know a great deal of detail about what your coachee actually wants to achieve, or you will describe something that doesn't fit, and interfere with his visualisation.

You may ask your coachee to describe what he sees, but again you need to be sensitive to what will help him visualise and what will interfere.

Finally, explore with your coachee how he can use his visualisation outside the coaching sessions.

I often use visualisation to help people become clearer about what they want. The 'script' I use is as follows, and it has proved quite powerful with both individuals and groups. I reproduce it here both because others might like to use it and also because it gives a sense of how a coach can help a coachee access his imagination. The script is called 'The Praise Party'.

The Praise Party

You may want to close your eyes as I take you through this exercise.

We are some time into the future and a new kind of organisational practice has become common. It is called the 'praise party.' You have been chosen to attend a praise party.

At this party, someone selected by you will talk to an assembled company, including many of your colleagues, friends and family, about you, your life, and your achievements.

You are notified of your praise party some three months before it happens, and then you choose the person who will speak about you; you don't talk to them at all about what they would say: people know the form.

Imagine who you would choose.

Now imagine that you are there, at your praise party. There are of course others there too who will be celebrated. You are standing with people you know and like well, sipping a glass of your favourite drink, in a beautiful room with a stage at the front.

A hush falls; the speeches are about to begin. You see the person you chose to speak about you walk across the stage and approach the lectern. They are about to speak.

What do you hope they will say?

At the end of this script, I just let people be quiet as they imagine for themselves their chosen person speaking in praise of them. It is often a good idea to ask people to write down what came to their minds, and of course it will be part of the next conversation.

Visualisation is a powerful way of increasing people's commitment to, and capability for, achieving their goals. But even more than many of the tools and techniques we have discussed in this part of the book, its success depends on the quality of the coaching relationship and process overall.

It depends on the coach having a good understanding of and rapport with his coachee. (I have come across coachees who hate to be the centre of attention, for example; the 'praise party' would not work for them at all.) It also depends on the coachee being sufficiently engaged with coaching to make the effort, both in the moment and over time, which successful use of visualisation depends on.

'Homework'

Of course, good coaching involves the coachee doing things between sessions as well as during them. But I want to explore here the importance of the coach setting 'homework' in terms of building the coachee's commitment to and capability for change.

Often a coachee will not know how committed and capable she is until she plans to do some homework. When she arrives at the next session, with her assignment undone, it provides invaluable information to coach and coachee. Maybe the 'wrong work' was suggested; in which case exploring why it was wrong will yield lots more information.

I remember a coachee of mine whom I asked to keep 'the morning pages' (see Chapter 14). She didn't, but instead began to write poems, which expressed her current feelings about her life and her hopes. The work I had set her was wrong, but it had started a train of thought that led to the 'right' work and an increasing sense of commitment to change.

> When the homework is done, like visualisation it represents an investment by the coachee in her own goals. That investment makes it more likely that she will persevere with them.

Maybe the homework isn't done because the goal at which the homework was directed is the wrong one.

An example of this is an executive who was asked by his coach to draw up a career development plan based on the themes they had been discussing. The executive arrived at the next session with no plan but a certainty that he wanted to leave his present company.

When the homework is done, like visualisation it represents an investment by the coachee in her own goals. That investment makes it more likely that she will persevere with them.

Building self-belief through internalising achievements

Of course, self-belief is the most important ingredient in commitment to and achievement of our goals. As Eleanor Roosevelt said, 'Whether you believe you can or whether you believe you can't, you're probably right.'

Adrian Moorhouse, world record-breaking swimmer and Olympic gold medallist, understands well that self-belief doesn't always follow naturally from great achievements. No matter what he achieved as a swimmer, he was always looking for the next thing.

When he broke the world record at the Commonwealth Games in 1990, for example, *The Times* journalist Simon Barnes asked him how he felt. He said: 'Disappointed, because I only equalled my previous time.' Barnes commented: 'You don't celebrate what you've done, you just look for the next mountain.'

Adrian recognised that this tendency of his – which many of us share even though our achievements may not be so remarkable – was not ideal if he wanted to build his self-belief and therefore his long-term commitment to and capability of achieving his goals. He ran into particular problems when he broke his wrist and couldn't swim for four months.

He was much in demand as a speaker, but found himself feeling 'a bit of a fraud'. Because he wasn't currently achieving as a swimmer, he felt as if he 'wasn't the person who does that anymore'. He hadn't internalised, and really taken possession of, his success.

So he knew when he retired from swimming, he had to spend some time internalising the successes he'd had, or he'd lose the confidence those successes had brought him. He describes this as one of the most important moments in his development, a moment that enabled him to leave swimming and move on to a very different kind of enterprise, that of running a business.

His self-belief needed to be on a solid foundation, and it was, once he had spent time with a coach taking stock of what he had achieved as a swimmer. He comments: 'I used to need to stoke the fire all the time with new wins; now it's permanently burning.'

Adrian has a coaching technique designed to help a coachee internalise her achievements and recognise her own successes and strengths.

He places a blank sheet of paper in front of his coachee, and draws eight big circles on it. He then invites her to think of things she has achieved (he may or may not specify a time frame) and write something in each of the circles. These things can be big or small (Adrian usually points out they don't have to include winning a gold medal!). They could be an achievement to do with family life, an example of a change someone has brought about by working on something identified to them in feedback, or an achievement in a hobby. They could be any mix of these and an infinity of others.

When his coachee has finished, she and Adrian look at the picture together. She can see what she's done.

Like most good techniques, this one is very simple. But it exploits the power of pictures (see the section on 'Diagrams and doodles' in Chapter 16). It is also very flexible. It can be used before an important event, something the coachee really needs to succeed at, or just as part of the general work of coaching. It can be left very open, with the coachee choosing anything at all to put in the circles, or it can be directed towards particular kinds of achievements. It can be used lots of times.

Setting goals and monitoring progress

It is worth referring back to Chapter 13 on goal-setting and Chapter 20 on monitoring progress. The techniques in both these chapters have a potentially big impact on the coachee's commitment and capability. In fact, if these two aspects of the work are done well, a coachee is two-thirds of the way to getting where he wants to be.

COACHING CONTEXTS

Introduction

The first four parts of this book have been about the foundations of all good coaching, wherever it occurs. Most of the examples and stories so far have been from my own context – that of a professional 'external' coach. They have also drawn heavily on experiences of one-on-one coaching, in order to get the principles clear with the simplest and most straightforward of illustrations.

In this part, Part Five, we move on to look at specific coaching contexts and explore the particular opportunities and challenges of those contexts. We explore how the foundations of good coaching can be applied when the coach is also the manager, and when it's a team rather than an individual that is being coached, and so on.

We have chosen the contexts that, from our experience, are most relevant to coaching at the moment. They are contexts in which people are often asked to coach yet where there are some significant and difficult issues to be dealt with if we are going to coach well.

Each chapter in this part of the book follows a similar format. It begins by introducing the coaching context, continues with identifying the key challenges and how to meet them, moves on to identifying the key opportunities and how to capitalise on them, with many examples of coaching in this context, and concludes with a summary of practical tips for applying the principles of good coaching in this context.

Chapter 21

The 'player-coach'

Introduction

Most managers are 'player-coaches', in a sense. They want, and often are required, to coach the people they work with but they also work alongside them. They share work goals with the people they coach, and their own success will be judged according to how well they and the people they coach meet their goals. The difference between coaching in this context and coaching as full-time role (that is, where the *only* relationship you have with a person is that of her coach) should not be underestimated. But it often is.

The view we shall take in this chapter, and justify, is that the principles of good coaching are much the same. But the barriers and leverage points to the successful execution of those principles are quite different.

In this chapter, we shall draw heavily on the experience of Brendan Venter. Having been a successful rugby player for South Africa at international level, Brendan was asked to play for and also be head coach for London Irish – a team based in London but representing the Irish who live and play rugby in England's capital. The intensity of playing and coaching rugby throws into sharp relief the opportunities and dilemmas of the player-coach. We shall explore them for insights that can serve the manager-coach as well.

It is worth making one point right at the start, however. Brendan was a successful player-coach. During his two years with London Irish, they significantly improved their ranking, winning a major trophy for the first time in the club's 104-year history and qualifying for the European Cup by finishing fourth in the league. Brendan was liked and respected by most of the people he worked with. But before he started in this dual role, other player-coaches said: 'You'd be mad to do it'. And, now his time in that dual role is over, Brendan says: 'Even in my first year, I knew it wasn't ideal – it's too much strain.'

So let's not underestimate the challenges, as we explore what the world of the player-coach has to teach us.

The challenges of visibility

The first challenge is that of visibility. Whereas a full-time coach is only seen by his coachee when he is coaching her, a player-coach is seen in many more settings. Not only that, his behaviour with other coachees will be visible to a particular individual. This places heavy demands on the coach

The coach must be, and be seen to be, consistent. And two kinds of consistency are involved. He must be treat all his coachees consistently. And his behaviour outside the coaching environment must continue to be consistent with the behaviour required of a coach.

If you recall the discussion in Part Two about the characteristics of effective coaches, you will remember that there are some fairly demanding requirements in terms of respect, integrity and appropriate motivation.

Brendan Venter says that if you are a player-coach, you have to live up to these standards in your play as well as in your coaching. He dealt with this challenge by having very clear and clearly articulated principles, which he always stuck to and which his fellow-players knew would always be applied. He also, and this is very interesting for the manager-coach, placed a huge emphasis on objective measures of performance.

He was known for the attention he paid to finding accurate and relevant measures and to applying them rigorously. For example, he would count how many times a player touched the ball, he would monitor heart-rate (and therefore work-rate) in training sessions, and he devised more complex statistics such as a measure of 'contribution to the team'.

Why did Brendan emphasise so strongly the importance of objective principles and measures? One reason must be that, as we have remarked, he needed to be, and to be seen to be, consistent and fair. He needed to be, and be seen to be, motivated by achieving the best result for his 'coachees'. He needed to provide evidence that he didn't act out of self-interest, and he needed his 'coachees' to judge him as having integrity, in the sense we described in Chapters 4 and 5. If his 'coachees' didn't judge him in that way, they wouldn't feel 'safe' with him (see Chapter 4) and he wouldn't be able to coach effectively.

photo: Michael Peel

Brendan Venter sets up an attack during the 2002 Powergen Cup Final

But Brendan couldn't be a saint. He is, like all of us, a mix of unselfish and selfish instincts, and his intentions will always be complex. So if he had just relied on generally behaving with integrity and respect, unmotivated by ego, and focusing on the common good, he would have been setting himself an impossible task. In the same way, a manager who thought that she needed to be saintly to be effective at coaching her people would probably give up immediately.

What Brendan had to do, and what managers who want to be taken seriously as coaches need to do, is establish a clear domain within which they will behave in accordance with the principles of good coaching. That domain is established through objective principles and measures. Coachees know exactly what they can expect. The objective principles and measures provide the transparency of motive and the evidence of intent that they need to benefit from coaching by their manager. The domain of those principles and measures is the domain within which the player/manager has credibility as a coach.

The challenge of mixed motives

Of course, the principles and measures have to correspond to the coachees' views on how they should behave and be measured. But once they are in place, the coachees will want to do well against them. That is then the agreed and transparent agenda for coaching, where the organisation's agenda and the individuals' agenda are at one (see the section on 'organisational motives' in Chapter 5).

So this approach also deals with another of the challenges for the player-coach and the manager-coach, that of mixed motives. The coachees may ask themselves – is she coaching me for my good or for her own good or for the organisation's good? The answer is, she is coaching me in order that I can do better according to our agreed principles and measures.

Of course, identifying and agreeing these principles and measures is not easy. The good news is, the manager-coach does not have to identify them all at the outset. It is helpful to be opportunistic and use the ones that most readily arise.

Much of the most effective coaching I have seen done by managers has, for example, occurred in response to feedback from clients. Both manager and staff readily agree that feedback from clients is important and that a key measure is how happy clients are. So their feedback provides a clear and agreed measure of

> Of course, the principles and measures have to correspond to the coachees' views on how they should behave and be measured. But once they are in place, the coachees will want to do well against them.

performance of the kind the manager-coach is looking for. Within that domain, the manager has credibility as coach.

It is also not easy to apply these principles and measures with absolute consistency. But coaching will be undermined if we don't. Brendan Venter tells the following story.

> 'I had a philosophy, and I told it to the team. I will never drop a player after one bad game, it had to be three, and he would be called in after every bad game so he knew how things stood. This was official policy.

'Then the team was going through a bad patch. One player had a small injury, and I substituted another. In that game, the team did fantastically (and it was down to the substitute, at least in part). I broke my rule. I announced the team with the new player in it.

'The player who was "dropped" came to me and said: "You said you would give us three chances." I realised he was so right. I looked him in the eyes and said: "I apologise. You will play this weekend."

'I went to the team and said I had made a mistake – although I knew the team would have been better with the new guy. The rest of the coaching staff said the team would be better with the new guy, but I said "It's irrelevant."

'The other player had not been playing badly, and the effect on my coaching of the team if I broke the principle would have been huge.'

The challenge of having more than just a coaching relationship with a coachee

For his entire time with London Irish, Brendan had a quote pinned up on the notice-board in his office.

It read: 'Having a clearly defined set of principles to work with reduces conflict because it depersonalises criticism. The players understand that the coach isn't attacking them personally when he corrects a mistake....' (The quote comes from *More Than a Game* by Philip Jackson and Charles Rosen (2002).) This quote brings us to another challenge for the player-coach and manager-coach, that of having more than just a coaching relationship with a coachee.

You may remember from Chapter 6 that one of the key skills in coaching is 'confronting'. Chapter 6 says: 'Sometimes it is the coach's job to turn up the heat, to generate some emotion that may provide the impetus for change.'

It's more problematic to take the decision to do that if there is a relationship outside of the coaching relationship that it is important for the coach to maintain. That is always true for a player-coach and a manager-coach. So it is particularly important to confront in a way that is not felt to be 'personal' by the coachee. Also the risk of her feeling a bit of confronting as personal is higher because of all the other interactions, apart from coaching, you have with her.

For example, perhaps yesterday she was grumpy around the office. Now today she is hearing some potentially useful but tough feedback from you. She may be asking herself: 'Is he just getting his own back for my grumpiness?'

So it is particularly important for coaches in this context to depersonalise their coaching by referring to objective standards.

Brendan Venter has another relevant and hard-hitting story to tell here.

> 'While I was at London Irish, I signed a player to come and work for us from South Africa. He was someone I knew well, a friend, as well as a good player. He packed up and moved his family over to London.

> 'His play went completely off the boil. All the performance indicators were terrible, and everyone knew. I treated him like everyone else, but he came to me and said I was being over-critical. But I was treating him the same way as everyone else, in line with our principles and measures.

> 'The board came to me with two people they wanted to let go. I said: "I will resign if you let the other guy go, he has fulfilled every performance indicator, but the guy who we brought over from South Africa, I back the decision to let him go."

> 'After the decision was announced he came to see me at my home. I told him I had backed the decision to let him go. He left, and he has never spoken to me since. I feel terrible about it, but if I had said "I wanted to keep you", it would have been a shocking lie. But I don't know if he and his family will ever speak to me again.'

So doing the right thing is no guarantee that you will not damage a relationship. It depends to some extent on factors in the other person that are outside your control.

This story helps us appreciate how real people's anxieties are when they need to raise difficult issues with those they hope to keep as friendly colleagues. But unless a player-coach sticks to objective and transparent standards, and confronts according to those, it is guaranteed that either his coaching or his relationships are likely to be seriously undermined.

The challenge of exhaustion

The size of task player-coaches take on can quite simply exhaust them. I do not only mean physical exhaustion, although that is part of it. I also mean exhaustion of emotional and mental resources.

Let's hear Brendan describe this exhaustion in his own words. It's a story keen followers of rugby may recognise.

'It was our fourth last match of the season. We played Bath; had we beaten them, we would have been mid-table and Bath would have been relegated. We would have been safe.

'We played well; it was a hard, physical game. We were two points ahead when I asked the ref "how long do we have left?" He said a minute.

"Bath got a scrum 40 metres from our line. Now, we hadn't conceded a try from such a position all season, but with half a minute left, they went for a try and got it. We lost.

'I have never in my life experienced two such extreme emotions in such close succession. From feeling confident and happy, 50 seconds later we find ourselves in a relegation battle. I was so dejected, I sat in the bus on the way home and just said "leave me alone".

'I sat for two days, then I got over it and said "OK, we'll fight again." But it was too much. It was one of the most disappointing moments of my entire life. I had worked incredibly hard for 79 minutes, and now this. It was almost the straw that broke the camel's back. I've been in relegation battles as just a coach, and as just a player, and it never ever hurt as much as it did that day. It was the combination that did it.'

(Just to complete the rugby story, London Irish ended up winning their last two matches comfortably and did avoid relegation.)

Brendan vividly communicates the double-whammy a player-coach experiences at times of failure. And then on top of that it is the coach's responsibility to help his colleague or colleagues respond effectively to that failure. Already reeling from the double blow of personal setback and a feeling of failure as a coach, the player-coach has to find the resources somewhere inside him to mobilise the others.

This is what managers face. They are told that they must coach as well as manage – and of course they must often do jobs of their own well too. What can they do to meet that challenge?

My view is they need coaching themselves. Who coaches the coaches? If an organisation is well organised around coaching, any boss who coaches will have his own boss to turn to for coaching. And when you get to the 'top of the pyramid' then there is a strong case for providing those people with external coaches. This won't make being a player-coach easy, but it will make it possible.

Many organisations are now following the principle that to increase the amount of coaching that goes on internally, you give top management external coaches on the basis that they will then coach their people, and the cascade will continue. That means that there is always support in place before a manager begins to coach his people. (It also of course means managers learn in the most effective way possible how to coach: by experiencing good coaching themselves.)

It is interesting that Brendan said that one of the factors that led him to accept the dual role was that he had a good relationship with his management. He felt they were his friends, and were behind him. Even at board level, he felt there was under-standing, if somewhat more distant. So maybe this was one reason that he was able to play and coach for as long as two years, and that he did it well. He too benefited from some informal coaching.

Who coaches the coaches? If an organisation is well organised around coaching, any boss who coaches will have his own boss to turn to for coaching.

Now let us look at some of the opportunities being a player-coach provides, and how to make the most of them.

The opportunity to coach by example

One of the biggest opportunities is that of coaching by example. Brendan Venter puts it like this: 'You can use yourself as the biggest coaching tool. You can get people to learn from mistakes without hurt-ing anyone's feelings. I used to look at myself on video and say "look at that mistake" – it was awesome when I did things wrong because that was the ultimate coaching tool.'

As Brendan also acknowledges, you have to be performing reasonably well yourself to turn your own mistakes into effective coaching oppor-tunities. It's unlikely a player-coach who is doing very badly on the field will have much credibility. But it's actually better if you're not too bril-liant.

(Brendan makes the interesting point that if you are too good you can perform without thinking about it, and that reduces your effec-tiveness as a coach. You lack understanding of what it means to strug-gle and try. He says: 'Very talented people don't have to explore the reasons for their success, and they don't know why other people don't get it.')

What is most effective of all is where you improve, and that improvement and the learning process that produced it are made obvi-ous to your coachees. The single most effective way of influencing another's behaviour is if a 'high-status' group member behaves in a certain way. Others are inclined to follow suit.

So if a boss (who is by definition 'high status' in the workgroup) can behave in a way that is clearly about continuous learning, openness about mistakes, and readiness to try something new even when it involves a bit of risk, then others are likely to follow suit, and that creates a climate in which coaching can be extremely effective.

Brendan also used his own learning to encourage people to identify their distinctive strengths and weaknesses. He would say: 'Notice I never kick the ball. Why not? Because I'm no good at kicking.' Then others could more easily acknowledge that there were aspects of their play that weren't so good. They could be encouraged to explore how to play to their strengths and get round their weaknesses.

(Brendan's view – and it is shared by many coaches both in sport and in business – is that you can work on your weaknesses, but improving your strengths often helps the team more.)

The opportunity to get your ego under control

You can readily appreciate that there isn't much opportunity for a player-coach with a big ego (that is, a need to demonstrate his own importance at the expense of others).

Brendan says: 'If you have in any way an ego, the first time you make a mistake you want to blame,' and then all the principles of good coaching fly straight out of the window.

So I think that being a player-coach or manager-coach offers a fantastic opportunity to get your ego under control. You will have to. Or you simply won't have any credibility as a coach. And that will hurt your ego! So being a player-coach is a good development programme for managers whose ego is getting in the way of their performance. But they would need very good coaching themselves first to prepare the ground!

The opportunity to show you really care

Probably the biggest opportunity that being a player-coach or manager-coach offers is the opportunity to show you really care. You share goals with your coachees, and you celebrate and suffer with them when things go well and badly. Also, without your having to prove it, your coachees see that you understand their world. You live in it too.

(That makes it important not to assume you understand an individual coachee's perspective, though; it will not necessarily be the same as yours, and so the questioning and active listening skills described in Chapter 6 are even more important.)

The opportunity to lift your own game

Finally, being a player-coach is an unparalleled opportunity to lift your own game.

Brendan talks about this in terms of his performance as a player. After all, that is where he started and playing will probably always be his first love. He says: 'Imagine how much I wanted to succeed at these measures I set; if I talked work-rate, how I wanted my work-rate to improve; if I talked "contribution to the team", how I would try at that, and so on.'

But being a player-coach is also a tremendous opportunity to raise your game as a coach. Because you have to apply all the principles of coaching but even more so, because of the constant (rather than periodic) demands on you to demonstrate respect for others, optimism and belief in others' potential, and integrity, and because you will get constant and immediate feedback on the effects of your coaching, it can make you or break you as a coach.

The opportunity to become more effective at working together

There is one last point that needs to be made about opportunity. Sports people don't make it, because in team sport team spirit is established by the very nature of the goals and the game. But in organisational life, where team spirit is so often needed and so often lacking, introducing coaching as part of a manager's day-to-day activity is a great opportunity for people in organisations to become more effective at working and learning together.

The principles and practices of effective coaching encourage people to invest in each other's success, to remove barriers to each other's achievement of potential, and to explore and understand the conditions for each other's excellence. They create an interpersonal glue that produces a more aligned and collegiate organisation.

Probably this is the reason why the role of manager as coach will continue to be highly valued in the world of business, despite Brendan saying from his perspective in the world of sport: 'The moment you become the boss, it's extremely hard to coach, ... you need to know what you are getting yourself into.'

Summary of practical tips for the 'player-coach'

1 Be very clear and very consistent in establishing and applying a set of principles you will follow as coach, and measures on which you will base evaluation of people's performance.

2 Apply all the principles of good coaching but even more so than would a full-time coach.

3 Accept that being a player-coach is difficult and make sure you have enough personal and professional resources to do it. Consider having a coach of your own to help you.

4 Be prepared for conflicts between what you want to do to keep a relationship sweet, and what you need to do as a coach.

5 Use yourself, and your own learning, as a primary tool in coaching. Model the kind of learning behaviour you want to see in others.

6 Watch out for making assumptions about the motives and situations of the people you coach. Use active listening and questioning even more than a full-time coach would.

7 If you can do something well without effort or thought, don't coach others in that area. If you have struggled to master something, see that as a good area to coach in.

8 Examine the size of your ego. If it is big, only go into coaching if you are committed to reducing it.

9 Use being a player-coach as a unique opportunity to develop your performance as a 'player' and as a coach. But don't be too hard on yourself. Allow yourself to make mistakes, to deviate from your principles; just remember to notice, and acknowledge what has happened with your people.

10 Examine your organisation's motives for asking you to coach. Only take it on if you are happy with them.

Chapter 22

Coaching teams

Introduction

There are whole books about teams and working with teams (some of which are referenced in the Bibliography at the end of this book). I myself have written two, and have also produced a resource pack of practical exercises for managers and facilitators to use when helping teams develop. So what are we hoping to achieve in a single chapter here on coaching teams?

First we hope to bring together insights from team coaching in the contrasting worlds of sport and business in a way that sheds some new light on the topic. So I shall again be making extensive reference to Brendan Venter's experience, coaching what many of us would consider the quintessential team activity: rugby.

I shall be exploring similarities and differences between his experiences and my experiences, in over 20 years of working with and coaching teams in business. I shall also draw on some of Adrian Moorhouse's insights as a swimmer coached for much of the time in the context of a 'squad' of other swimmers (see Chapter 3) and as a 'player-coach' leading a company.

The second thing we hope to achieve is, as in the previous chapter, to identify how the principles of coaching we have laid out in this book so far can be applied to teams, and what the distinctive challenges and opportunities are. In short, this chapter should enable the reader to take the whole book and use it to inform not just one-to-one but also team coaching.

We need to be clear about what kind of team coaching we are addressing here. In sport, the objective of team coaching is clear and understood by all: to enable the team to win, and to increase its chances of winning over time. In business, we are not blessed with such clarity and simplicity.

Of course, one purpose of team coaching is to enable the team to succeed at a particular objective. But more usually the focus is on enabling the team, and also the individuals within it, to 'develop'. The assumption is that a 'developed' team will be more successful than a less developed one, but the focus of coaching tends to be on development itself rather than on 'success', which is much more difficult to agree and measure in business than in sport.

In this difference lie some of the most important differences between sports team coaching and business team coaching. We shall look at those differences and their implications in the paragraphs that follow. For now, let us just be clear that we are talking about both coaching for team performance and coaching for team development, that the two are connected but not simply so, and that where the differences are important we shall discuss them explicitly.

Let us look now at the particular challenges of team coaching, and how to meet them.

The challenge of establishing a focus for coaching

The first challenge of team coaching in business results directly from the difference from sports coaching we have just described. It is the challenge of establishing a focus for coaching transparent to and agreed by the team. In one-to-one coaching, this is achieved mainly through the goal-setting process described in Part Four. In sports coaching, as we have said, the focus is obvious. In business team coaching, things are more complex.

What the coach of a team needs to have is an idea in her mind of what a development path for the team looks like, and what distinguishes effective from ineffective team performance. The simpler this idea is the better, because it will be easier for her to apply it and because it will be easier for her to share it with the team.

There are a number of models of team development to choose from (Belbin's being the most well-known: see Belbin 1993); the important thing is for the coach to have and to communicate the one she is happy with.

My own mental model is based on two background theories: Schutz's framework for understanding the needs people have in relation to others (you may remember this framework was discussed in full in Part Three), and the insights achieved by the French psychoanalyst W.R. Bion into what enables people to form an effective work group (see Bion 1961).

So, following Schutz, I am directing my coaching at issues of *inclusion* (do people feel sure they belong in the team? Are roles clear in the team, and are they appropriate?), of *control* (is the role of the leader working well? Are decisions made in an effective and appropriate way?), and of *openness* (is the team sharing the information it needs to? Are people able to give each other feedback? Do people feel they are valued in the team?).

I am aiming to increase the capability of the team to deal with all these issues themselves.

Following Bion, I am also directing my coaching at issues of clarity of purpose (are people clear and agreed about what the team needs to do? Are all team members committed? At this moment, are they clear and agreed on the purpose of this conversation?)

Another way of formulating the guiding focus for team coaching is through 'ground rules'. I mostly use ground rules based on Senge's 'rules for skilful discussion' (see Senge et al 1994) and Schwarz's ground rules from *The Skilled Facilitator* (2002). Here is a summary of the set I use:

- agree the purpose of conversations, and keep it in mind
- share all relevant information
- build shared meaning; clarify and give examples
- balance advocacy and enquiry
- discuss the 'undiscussable' (the 'elephant in the corner')
- stay aware of feelings and use the information they provide.

Again, the coach needs to be explicit that she will be intervening to develop the team's capability to work together according to these ground rules.

The important point here is not that a particular mental model is the right one, although if you read the references above you will see that they have strong similarities to each other and that there is good and reasonably rigorously researched understanding now of how people work most effectively together. But the important point is you must have a mental model, the team must know what it is, and they must agree it is appropriate.

The important point is you must have a mental model, the team must know what it is, and they must agree it is appropriate.

Having said that things are different in sports team coaching, it is interesting to hear from Brendan that they may not be as different as all that.

While coaching London Irish, he took the view that his coaching needed to focus on performance, not results. Only by articulating and agreeing with the team a set of objective performance measures could he coach them effectively (examples of these measures are given in the previous chapter).

In other words, he had to establish a focus for coaching transparent to, and agreed by, the team. Because of all the variables he couldn't control, focusing on results wouldn't have got the team where it needed to get to.

Of course, it was relatively easy for the rugby team to see the relationship between the behaviours Brendan's performance measures focused on and the possibility of a winning result. It is harder for business teams to see the relationship between, for example, the behaviour 'discuss undiscussable issues' and the result of reducing costs across the company by 10 per cent. And in fact they will probably have to take some of their coach's recommendations for the focus of coaching on trust, and on evidence of her previous success with teams.

The challenge of complexity

A second challenge of coaching teams is the sheer complexity of what you have to attend to. It is the mental model of the focus of coaching that helps again here. It guides you to attend to behaviours that will cause the greatest improvement in performance, and that are under the team's control. It gives you as the team coach a structure and a discipline, which in turn reduces your anxiety and makes you more useful to the team.

The challenge of group dynamics

Because another challenge of team coaching is the power of group dynamics. (By 'group dynamics' I mean all the invisible and emotional forces and communications between individuals in a group, which lead groups to behave in much more extreme ways than any of the individuals would have done on their own.)

There is always the potential for strong and destructive emotion in teams. Here, sport and business are the same. (Although in business people are more reluctant to express those emotions openly.)

Brendan talks about the jealousy and rivalry in a rugby team, and the fact that these strong emotions can result in actual physical attacks, in training and in the match. I have seen jealousy and rivalry lead to blistering and humiliating verbal attacks in the boardroom, and I have seen such emotion lead to cruel and sustained campaigns to get rid of particular individuals. Physical attack is probably easier to recover from than this, or, as Brendan puts it – and he would know – 'Words hurt more than a kick in the face.'

To coach a team when these kinds of powerful emotion are in train is hard. The coach will feel the power of the emotion, as a fellow human being, and may become very anxious. What the coach needs is a way of maintaining his emotional distance whilst remaining close as a coach.

It is interesting that Brendan is a very independent-minded and personally courageous individual. As a child growing up in South Africa, he learned to take a stand against apartheid even though there were considerable emotional pressures on him not to. He has a very strong and well-developed set of values by which he lives the whole of his life. He has, in other words, something that holds him apart from the power of particular group dynamics even while he is absolutely committed to working with the group.

The same kind of personal courage and forcefulness is also evident in a story Adrian tells about his first swimming coach.

The squad of swimmers had started to be very negative, 'the pool's too cold', 'the public swimmers are getting in our way', and so on. Adrian's coach came in one day and said: 'No more negative comments.'

He was fed up with it, but also he probably knew that a culture of negativity would not help anyone's development as a swimmer. He sent anyone who made a negative comment home immediately.

At the end of the coaching session, there were two left out of 20! He continued in the same way over subsequent sessions; four lasted till the end of the second session; but by the end of the week the swimmers had got the message.

Three of the most negative had left altogether, but the rest of the squad continued in a much more positive atmosphere. The coach had forced a behavioural change, which then became a habit, and finally laid the foundation for a belief and a value. The remaining squad became focused on positivity and success.

When a coach works with a business team, he too needs a strong set of values and principles that are more important to him than approval or belonging. He needs to have worked out what these are.

And if the group dynamic in a team is very powerful and very destructive, it may be better for coaching to be done by a team of two coaches working together. It is much easier to resist the power of group dynamics when there is more than one of you.

It is interesting that for team sports there is usually a team of coaches. Part of the reason for that is the team needs coaches with different specialisms, but of course it also means that the head coach is 'stronger' because he has back-up and support (providing the coaching team is working well itself!)

The challenge of balancing team and individual needs

The final challenge of team coaching I want to look at here is that of coaching many individuals together. Although the focus of coaching is on team performance, the team is composed of individuals, and it will be the combined effect of many changes in individuals' behaviour that will lead to team development or team disintegration.

How can the team coach intervene in a way that responds to the different personalities and is still seen as fair? How can the team coach get the balance right between individual needs and the team's needs?

Let's look first at some of Brendan's experiences. First, he acknowledges that 'in rugby there is no opportunity to be successful without the other guys.' So even if someone is primarily personally driven, he will invest in the team, because that is the only way he's going to get what he wants.

In contrast, and just as an example, I was coaching a management team recently each of whose members was himself responsible for a large chunk of the business. They had not worked together effectively on the development and communication of a new strategy, and it became clear that they had been 'too busy looking after their own patches'. They could experience lots of success without any investment in this team at all.

So a coach needs to work with the team to ensure that every team member (in the words of a New Zealand businessman I worked with) has some 'skin in the game'.

Second, Brendan talks passionately about the so-called 'disruptive influences' in a team (when he played in South Africa, he was considered to be one!).

He says that highly individually driven and hence 'difficult' team members are often the biggest 'responsibility-takers'.

In other words, once their individualistic behaviour has been contained with a set of clear and consistent rules that they can see the sense of, then they will work harder than anyone to get themselves and the team to improve.

Such individuals feel threatening to a coach, because they do not readily comply, they question and challenge, they ask themselves all the time 'what's in it for me?' But both they and the team will benefit if the coach can help them achieve respect.

In my experience, it's the same in business teams. Strong individualists are hard to work with. But once their commitment to the team is elicited, they are likely to play a major part in driving the team's performance forward. So they are worth extra coaching effort, from the team's point of view.

Although the coach may spend more time with, and appear to pay more attention to, some team members than others at different stages of the team's development, what needs to be absolutely consistent is the focus of coaching. In other words, the same basic rules of performance apply to everyone.

Schwarz has something that is particularly important to say on this topic of dealing with all the individual interests within the context of the team. In his classic text *The Skilled Facilitator*, he writes: '[A key principle] is treating the entire group as the client rather than only the formal group leader.' What a coach must keep at the forefront of his mind is that everyone in the team is equally important, and that it is the team as a whole whose interests he is addressing.

Adrian has an interesting extra perspective on this, as a consequence of the way swimmers are coached in groups. In this case, the group doesn't have an overarching 'team purpose'; they are not a team and will not compete as such; but it is important for all of their individual success that they work together well.

Adrian says the key is 'respect' on the part of the coach (see Chapter 4) for all the individuals. What this means in this context is that the coach has to believe in the potential of each member of the group, and has to know that he doesn't know who will be best.

He also has to be able to 'look beyond behaviour' and go on believing in each individual's potential. Someone may be tired or stroppy, but the coach has to look beyond that and stay focused on the whole person and her capabilities.

Once again, we see that the key to successful coaching lies at the level of the values and beliefs of the coach. A coach must be, in Adrian's words, 'true to themselves'; and belief in someone else cannot be faked.

In sport and in business, that sometimes means an individual team member should leave because her impact on the team is too destructive. Brendan says the people who need to leave are those who are in the 'I'm not OK, you're not OK' life position (see Chapter 3). He says: 'You have to get rid of them because they try to bring other people down.' The emphasis has to be on creating a positive environment; 'that's a non-negotiable in sport', says Brendan.

In sport, a team coach will have an important say on team composition, and it will be part of his job to recruit and dismiss team members. In business, a team leader who is also coaching his team may or may not have a similar authority.

> What a coach must keep at the forefront of his mind is that everyone in the team is equally important, and that it is the team as a whole whose interests he is addressing.

An external coach to a team is very unlikely to take any part in recruitment or dismissal – and it would compromise the main benefits of having an external coach if he did. When a team member is destructive, and has to stay, the important thing for the coach to do is help the team learn how to minimise the effects of that destructiveness.

The task of the coach is also to stay focused on the difficult individual as a person and hold on to her belief in that individual's potential, while helping the team cope with the destructive behaviours. The coach will do the former by spending time with the individual one-to-one, and the latter helping the team to learn and apply the principles and ground rules of effective team working.

Now let us look at the undeniable opportunities that team coaching presents.

The opportunity for extra insight as a coach

One of the opportunities it is most important for a team coach to capitalise on is the upside of one of the biggest challenges we have just discussed. It is connected with the power of group dynamics.

Because the feelings generated and communicated by groups are so powerful, and resonate with underlying hopes and fears in all of us, when there are feelings getting in the way of teamwork, the team coach is likely to feel it too. So she has the opportunity for using her own feelings as coach to understand what is blocking the team.

Here is an example. I was working with a management team to help them develop a shared understanding of the values they wanted to underpin and guide their business practices. The team's leader had had to cancel his attendance at the last minute because of a family emergency, but had asked that the meeting should go ahead in his absence.

After an hour or so working with the team, I began to feel anxious. I began to be preoccupied with whether I was doing a good job, and whether the team would ask me to work with them again. I felt like putting a lot more energy into trying to get the team to some conclusion so I could feel satisfied that we had accomplished something. But at the same time I felt nothing I might do would make a difference.

Fortunately, I managed to get some objectivity about my feelings. Instead of staying mired in my own despondency, I thought perhaps my feelings were telling me something important about the team.

I asked the team how they thought the meeting was going, and of course discovered a whole range of feelings in them that were blocking their performance. They were angry the leader wasn't there, angry that this work on values might be overturned by him after they had done it, and depressed because they had tried to agree values twice previously and it hadn't resulted in any lasting practical benefit.

My feelings had alerted me to some important issues for the team, which they needed my help as coach to deal with.

This is just one example. I have hundreds, both from my experience as coach and from observing team leaders, who aspire to coach their teams, failing to use the feelings they undoubtedly have during meetings (you can hear them in their tone of voice, see them in their body posture and skin colour) as information about something important in the team that needs to be addressed.

It is hard to use our feelings as information, particularly when those feelings are strong. But if as team coaches we don't, we miss out on one of the biggest leverage points for coaching we have in that context. Not only that, but our own feelings and their effects will become additional blocks to team development and effectiveness.

The opportunity for peer coaching

A second opportunity it is worth exploring is that of getting team members to coach each other. The best changes a coach can bring about for a team are improvements in the ability of team members to give each other feedback, intervene to get the best out of each other, and ultimately become a 'self-coaching team'.

For the coach is only with the team some of the time (and in sport, is only there for training, not during the actual game!), and if the team are dependent on her interventions they will not perform at their potential best.

So the more a coach can ask the team first for views on how to take things forward, on how things are going, on what's going well and badly, and coach team members in ways of giving those views constructively, the more the team will develop.

Interestingly, Brendan acknowledges he has a problem with this aspect of coaching. He says: 'My biggest problem as a coach is, I am so dominant, I have problems getting the team to talk to each other.' But he has worked hard on this, recognising its importance. He has found that if he keeps quiet when one team member is offering important tips to another, it implies 'his blessing' and increases the impact of the advice.

The opportunity for direct observation

The last opportunity in team coaching we shall draw attention to here is perhaps the most obvious. It is the opportunity for observing performance directly.

Unlike one-to-one coaching, where performance tends to happen outside the coaching environment, a team coach, particularly in business, sees performance happening as she coaches. The opportunity for learning in the here-and-now (in many people's view, the most effective kind of learning of all) is there to be capitalised on.

As in all feedback, that opportunity has to be used with skill. It is particularly important for the coach to distinguish between observations of behaviour and conclusions she is drawing from that behaviour. She may say: 'You didn't stick to the plan you had for managing the time.' She would be ill-advised to say: 'You are finding it hard to accept Jo's authority,' for example.

For one thing, her inference might well be wrong, and be a red herring for them. For another, it robs the team of the opportunity to investigate among them whether anything significant is going on and what they should do about it.

In fact, when coaching a team, the best approach to learning in the here-and-now is to create the environment where that will happen and let the team members decide what they need to coach each other on.

A coach can do this by asking open questions – how are things going? What's on your minds? – and by putting in place more structured opportunities for reviewing team performance.

With all the interactions that go on in a team, it is an extremely rich learning environment, potentially. Individuals will learn a great deal from being part of a well-coached team, and one of the most productive coaching contexts I have worked with capitalises on this fact. It happens when coaching is provided not just to the team as a whole, but by the same coach to all the individual team members on a one-to-one basis. Of course, that opportunity is open to all team leaders who coach, although as we said in the last chapter, there are significant challenges to doing so successfully as a 'manager-coach'.

Summary of practical tips for the team coach

1 Be very clear in your own mind about the purpose of the coaching: is it to enable a particular piece of high performance by the team? Is it to develop the team generally?

2 Find a framework, model and/or set of ground rules to guide your coaching. Make it explicit and agree with the team that it is appropriate.

3 Accept that sometimes the group dynamics will be so powerful that you are at a loss. Get a coach yourself, or consider working in a coaching 'team'.

4 Be very clear that your client is the whole team, and not any individual more than any other. Behave consistently and according to your ground rules with everyone in the team.

5 Look out for 'individualists'. They may be the hardest work, but have the most potential as 'responsibility-takers'.

6 Ensure that every team member has sufficient 'skin in the game'.

7 Stay aware of what you are feeling as you coach the team, and use your feelings as a source of information about what is going on in the team.

8 Coach team members to coach each other; this capability will be of more long-lasting benefit than any number of 'brilliant' coaching interventions by the coach.

9 Put in place opportunities for the team to review its own performance.

10 Use what you see directly in the team's behaviour to coach in 'real-time' but do so with all the skills required for effective feedback (see Part Four).

Chapter 23

'Corridor coaching'

Introduction

Some of the most effective coaching happens in short opportunistic exchanges rather than in longer planned sessions or as part of a formal coaching programme. This is good news from a manager-coach's point of view, and also good news from an organisational point of view. Coaching is often seen as a heavy burden on people who are already busy; it need not be so.

But before taking advantage of such informal and brief coaching opportunities, it is as well to be aware of the challenges.

The challenge of spotting the opportunity

In Chapter 1 we introduced the idea of 'breakdowns' in specific relation to coaching opportunities: times when the path we are on becomes blocked or difficult to follow, and we are open to something from outside the normal flow of things to help us continue. With more formal and planned coaching, the coachee will often have identified such a 'breakdown' for herself and she will arrive at coaching with an agenda ('I need to improve my presentation skills'; 'I need to manage my team differently'). Even when she doesn't, there is plenty of time within the formal coaching process to explore what the 'breakdown' might be.

But in 'corridor coaching' the opportune moments have to be seized and there isn't, by definition, much time. Here are some contexts in which a quick bit of coaching may be just what a colleague needs. Read these so that you can begin to develop your 'antennae' for those good corridor coaching moments:

- your colleague has just done, or is about to do, something for the first time
- your colleague has just done, or is about to do, something she sets a lot of store by

- your colleague has just had something go badly
- your colleague has just had something go remarkably well.

But probably the key to spotting these opportunities lies in your awareness of your own response to the situation. If you have seen or heard something, and you feel you could help, then maybe you can.

I remember, for example, facilitating a meeting where I observed that the team leader did not look at one of her team members once during the first two hours. She looked at the others, and the individual she wasn't looking at addressed an increasing number of remarks and questions to her directly, but she never met his gaze.

At the break, I found the team leader in her office, and decided a bit of 'corridor coaching' might be a good idea. I felt that by encouraging her to reflect on how she had felt, how she had behaved, and what she wanted to achieve in the meeting, I might help her have a more effective second half to the meeting.

If you are constantly on the look-out for ways to opportunities to help people achieve their goals more effectively, you will find them.

The challenge of being sure that it's a good time

However, therein lies another challenge of 'corridor coaching'. Just because the opportunity is there, it doesn't mean the potential coachee wants to be coached, or can in fact benefit from coaching at that time. And coaching given to someone who doesn't want it or can't benefit from it for some other reason (as we explored at some length right at the beginning of this book) is often a waste of time and sometimes downright destructive.

In the example I just described, did the team leader want coaching from me in the break? Maybe she had other things to do; maybe she was too angry and set on a particular course of action to be coached; maybe she knew exactly what she was doing and why, and didn't need any contribution from me. Maybe any number of things: 'people are always and already in the middle of their lives' (Flaherty 1999). They have things going on, inside them and outside them, which only they know about.

Just because the opportunity is there, it doesn't mean the potential coachee wants to be coached, or can in fact benefit from coaching at that time.

What if I, as a coach, have just seen the 'perfect' opportunity for a well-timed and carefully guided bit of reflection, for example? That is because I am in 'the middle of' coaching. But they are in the middle of something quite different, and coaching may or may not be what they need.

So we have to ask permission to coach, as we described in Chapter 1. We may be short of time, but it's the most important bit of 'corridor coaching', and it's the bit most commonly left out.

Think about the manager who launches straight into a review of his colleague's performance at a key client presentation in the car on the way back from the meeting. His colleague is preoccupied with the revised proposal he has to write now to a tight deadline, and also hungry because he skipped breakfast to get to the meeting in time, and also annoyed with his manager because he kept interrupting him in the meeting. Coaching is not going to work well.

How do we ask permission? The most straightforward way is best. We can simply ask questions such as: 'Would you like to spend a few minutes talking with me about any of this? Is there any way I can help you plan/ review this? Is now a good time to talk about what went well and what went badly there?'

But be careful to be ready to accept the answer 'no'. And don't structure your question in a way that makes it almost impossible for your colleague to say 'no'. 'Would you like to hear my view on the one thing you did that ruined that meeting?' is not a good permission-seeking question, for example.

The challenge of avoiding advice

Another challenge of 'corridor coaching' is that of resisting the temptation to give advice. Advice is not coaching. It limits rather than extends the range of possibilities open to the coachee. It does not take into account what the coachee is 'already in the middle of'. It does not empower the coachee, and it implies there is a fairly straightforward solution but the coachee hasn't seen it. That is disrespectful.

If I had, for example, said to the team leader I talked about earlier in this chapter, 'I advise you to look at John more in the second half of the meeting,' that advice could have trivialised the strength of her feelings during the meeting (which she knew meant she couldn't look at John without glaring), it could have led her to follow a red herring (to focus on how she looks at John rather than on what she needs to get out of the meeting) and so on.

It could have had any number of unhelpful consequences. And the very fact of my saying it might have demonstrated that I had little understanding of what was really going on, from her point of view.

But when we feel pressured by time, we often, and unconsciously, switch into advice-giving. I have seen this time and again with managers on training courses.

One recently was heard saying to a colleague whom he was coaching (in order to develop his own coaching skills!), 'I know I shouldn't give you advice, but what I really think you should do is ...'

In 'corridor coaching', we are by definition short of time. How can we resist the urge to give advice? My recommendation to people is that they try to cultivate more curiosity. If you see an opportunity to coach a colleague, get curious. What does the situation look like to your colleague? How does she feel about it? What does she want to achieve? What kind of help would she welcome from you?

Another challenge of 'corridor coaching' is that of resisting the temptation to give advice. Advice is not coaching.

I think we find it hard to believe that being understood has a more positive effect on our ability to live life as we want to than does any amount of well-intended instruction. But if we are going to take effective advantage of 'corridor coaching' we each have to find our own way of keeping that belief at the forefront of our minds.

If we do that, we are in a good position to capitalise on the opportunities 'corridor coaching' provides.

The opportunity to make efficient use of time

If journeys to and from client sites, a few minutes here and there before and after meetings, chats over coffee and at the beginning and ends of days, can be made to work as times for coaching, then the amount of coaching can be greatly increased without increasing the time burden on managers and their people.

Confidentiality, and hence privacy, are still key, but any time when two colleagues are together without some pressing work goal that they need to accomplish immediately is a time when coaching could happen. Also, coaching can be woven into other work.

A manager I worked closely with used to punctuate one-on-one working sessions with his staff with the question 'Anything in all of this you have concerns about?' This could often lead to a bit of opportunistic coaching. Or that even simpler but even less used question 'How do you feel about this?' is another good way of creating an opening.

The opportunity to give immediate feedback

So long as we don't bypass the permission-seeking bit of coaching, and we are genuinely open to the possibility that someone won't find feedback from us helpful right now, 'corridor coaching' opens the door to some of the most effective feedback people may ever receive.

We see someone lose their temper in a meeting; we ask them after the meeting if they would value some feedback on how they came across; they say they would. Now while the situation is fresh in both our minds we can explore what triggered the red face and raised voice, what the effects were, whether those effects were consistent with what the individual wanted to achieve, and what he could do differently.

I am often in the position of helping coachees 'reconstruct' moments like this days or even weeks after they have happened. It is hard for them to remember accurately exactly what happened, and their learning is less as a result.

Of course, if you are also the manager of the person you are considering giving feedback to, you may need to give that feedback however unwelcome it is as part of your management responsibility. If a deadline will be missed or a client relationship damaged unless that person changes, you need to tell him so. But that is different from looking for coaching opportunities.

This distinction can seem a bit subtle to managers and coachees alike, and is of course connected with the general difficulties of being a 'player-coach' (see Chapter 21). The best we can hope to do is be direct and honest – with ourselves first, and our colleague next – about why we are giving feedback.

There is, for example, a difference between saying 'I need to talk to you about the last meeting with the client because I think we may have a problem', and 'Is there anything about that last meeting with the client which you'd like some feedback from me on?'

The opportunity for culture change

The final opportunity of 'corridor coaching' I want to bring to your attention is a powerful one indeed. It is the opportunity for changing the culture of the organisation.

'Corridor coaching', once people have practised it and are used to it, becomes much more natural and effortless than formal coaching. Of course, formal coaching sessions are always needed for big and complex issues, so I am not saying 'corridor coaching' can replace them. But because of the spontaneity of 'corridor coaching' and the way it is woven into the rest of organisational life, it has the potential to become just part of 'the way things are done around here'. And that is the definition of culture (Schein 1992).

'Corridor coaching' can spread rapidly through an organisation if a few 'high-status' individuals start to practise it. I have seen that happen in small and fairly flat organisations such as investment houses and niche management consultancies. Here the 'high-status' individuals are often the ones who do the best work, and the quality of their work is pretty visible to everyone in the company.

> The final opportunity of 'corridor coaching' I want to bring to your attention is a powerful one indeed. It is the opportunity for changing the culture of the organisation.

They tend not to be so keen on a large amount of formal coaching sessions because the organisation itself is informal. Also, they tend to view with suspicion anything time-consuming that takes them away from their clients. But where they start making the most of informal opportunities to help colleagues grow and develop, this has a profound impact on their organisation's culture and performance.

In a piece of research I conducted a few years ago for a major European investment bank, I discovered that parts of the bank had just such a culture, and the prevalence of 'corridor coaching' (although they didn't call it that) was the single biggest reason why high performers stayed with the bank.

Summary of practical tips for the 'player-coach'

1 Pay close attention to what is going on in your colleagues' working lives so that you can identify, in time to make use of them, times when a bit of coaching from you might help them.

2 Never assume that coaching will be welcome, from you, at this time, in this situation. Remember that people are 'always already in the middle of something'.

3 Ask for an invitation to coach. If none is forthcoming, don't coach.

4 Remember that if you feel short of time, you will probably coach more directively than usual, and that may well not be effective.

5 Don't give advice under the label of coaching. Cultivate curiosity in yourself as an antidote to inappropriate advice-giving.

6 Make the most of time when you and a colleague are alone. Time travelling together in a car is particularly promising.

7 Make the distinction between coaching and management clear, if you are also the individual's manager.

8 Make observations about your colleagues' behaviour and performance that they could learn from. Look for opportunities to give immediate feedback, or encourage reflection on something that has just happened.

9 Don't give this feedback unless your colleague asks for it.

10 Look for ways in which corridor coaching can become more prevalent in your organisation; it is a real opportunity for culture change. Talk about the fact that you do it, or have experienced it.

Chapter 24

Building a 'coaching culture'

Introduction

We have talked already in this book about the value of a coach encouraging and enabling team members to coach each other (Chapter 22, 'Coaching teams'). And in the last chapter we have observed how 'corridor coaching' can spread to become an important influence on the culture of an organisation.

In this chapter we want to take that thought a step further. So many organisations are interested in establishing just such a coaching culture, yet they find it difficult. (By 'coaching culture' they mean not a culture where everyone has an external coach, but a culture where people coach each other all the time as a natural part of meetings, reviews and one-to-one discussions of all kinds.)

There are commercial and competitive pressures in organisations that go against the grain of coaching's fundamental principles. So in this chapter we intend to examine how a leader who is personally committed to coaching can establish a coaching culture in her organisation, addressing the very real challenges, and capitalising on the equally real opportunities.

In this chapter, we shall take Adrian Moorhouse and his company, Lane 4, as a reference point. For reasons that will become clear as the chapter progresses, Adrian is not a typical business leader and Lane 4 is not a typical company. We shall acknowledge the distinctive and unusual characteristics of Adrian and Lane 4, as we highlight what works for them, and the difficulties they still struggle with, and draw out the learning points for organisations generally.

Before we start, we need to paint a brief picture of Adrian and his company. (Adrian has of course already featured several times in this book, in his role as world record-breaking swimmer and Olympic gold medallist. Here we are focusing on his current role as managing director of a company with 45 full-time staff and almost as many associates.)

Lane 4 is a consultancy dedicated to the improvement of individual, team and organisational performance in its clients. Many of its staff have a sports or sports psychology background, and in addition to its consultancy work it has a research team led by one of Adrian's partners.

So two big differences between Adrian and Lane 4, and the vast majority of other organisations, are immediately apparent.

First, because of his personal background, as someone whose sporting success was, in his own words, 'a lot to do with the coaching I had', Adrian is profoundly committed to coaching as a means to improve performance. Few leaders of organisations have had either Adrian's experience of a wide range of coaching styles and their effects, or the deep development over time of a belief in the value of coaching.

Second, Lane 4 has the provision of coaching to its clients at the centre of its business, as both formal individual or team coaching, and informal coaching as a natural by-product of their consultancy style. So Lane 4 knows that by committing to a coaching culture internally it is 'practising what it preaches', and that is good for business.

It is good for business not only because the business performs better; it is good for business because there is a consistency between what Lane 4 people do, and what they advise others to do. By committing to a coaching culture themselves, they are doing business in a way that is true to what they are.

These two distinctive characteristics of our case study lead us straightaway into a clear insight into two of the biggest challenges for most organisations in establishing a coaching culture.

The challenge of changing attitudes

The widespread and high-profile use of coaching in the business context is a relatively recent phenomenon. Most current business leaders have got where they are today without a coach's help (at least, a coach in the formal sense). Not only that, in business it is often seen as a weakness to attribute some of your success to someone else's help.

This is very different from the world of sport, where it is taken for granted that a good coach will help even the most naturally talented of performers achieve more of their potential. Sportspeople tend to be proud of their coaches. Business people can be slightly embarrassed, and wonder if their having a coach will detract from their image of having done it all by themselves.

This attitude is probably the biggest barrier to establishing a coaching culture. We mentioned briefly in the last chapter that 'corridor coaching' was likely to spread where 'high status' individuals started doing it. As with most things in organisational life, it is what the leaders (both formal and informal) do that influences others, not what they say.

So to establish a coaching culture in an organisation where the people with most power don't have coaching themselves, or have it secretly, is very hard work and may not be possible.

I was invited to offer coaching to the partners of a medium-sized firm of lawyers many years ago. I insisted that the managing partner had coaching himself, to make it possible for his colleagues to take it up. He was puzzled; he genuinely wanted this help to be available to his partners, but felt no need of it himself.

I knew that at that time, and in that highly competitive culture, having coaching would be seen as a sign of weakness unless the most powerful person in the firm led the way. (He did, found it useful – to his surprise – and talked about it openly to his colleagues. As a consequence, that firm became the first law firm I know to establish coaching as a norm for its partners. Sadly, when that managing partner left, and was replaced by someone who didn't value coaching, the take-up of coaching faded away.)

With Adrian at the head of Lane 4, the most significant barrier to establishing a coaching culture has already been overcome. And of course it is not only in his past life as a sportsman that he has valued coaching. He seeks coaching from his fellow partners, the team more broadly, and a handful of trusted 'outsiders'.

The message 'coaching is a normal part of what successful people do around here' is communicated loud and clear. For anyone wanting to establish a coaching culture, that is the message that has to be got across. And it will be got across by actions, not words.

The challenge of reconciling business goals with coaching goals

The second challenge that Lane 4 is particularly well placed to overcome is that of the perceived conflict between the demands of coaching and the needs of the business. For most organisations, the link between a coaching culture and the business they are in has to be proved. It is not immediately apparent. Many influential people will take the view that coaching is a good idea, but getting on with the 'real business' has to come first.

Whereas for Lane 4, coaching is an intrinsic part of the real business, it can seem like a luxury to organisations driven by the need to sell quite other products and services.

The only way to meet this challenge is with evidence. Examples of how coaching has resulted in an increase in both individual and organisational performance must be identified and talked about. And the best examples are found in the organisation's own experiences. There are plenty of books and papers giving general evidence of the link between coaching and performance. But every organisation believes itself to be unique; it needs examples and proof from its own industry and, preferably, from its own people, to take things seriously.

Lane 4 has now had the experience of sticking with its coaching culture and not only surviving but growing through the recent recession. That builds confidence. The challenge is to persuade an organisation to try the investment of time and effort so that it can find out for itself whether it works.

The challenge of communicating

A related challenge is the difficulty of communicating exactly what a 'coaching culture' is. Again, Lane 4 has an advantage. The many sports people and sports psychologists working there are already familiar with working environments where a high level of coaching is the norm.

But for many business people, they hear that a coaching culture is a good idea, that it will improve morale, ensure talented people stay, and encourage the full realisation of the organisation's long-term potential, but they don't know exactly what it means. What would be different about their organisation if it had such a thing?

I asked Adrian what a visitor to Lane 4 would notice that marks the company out as having a coaching culture. He described a lot of different things:

- the large number of cross-company teams, whose composition is based on individual interests and passions as much as on expertise
- the leadership of those teams: the person with the most energy is the person who leads, irrespective of company position

- the atmosphere of those teams, an atmosphere of openness and respect for and interest in everyone's views
- a lot of coaching of staff by other members of staff; a 'Lane 4 does Lane 4' philosophy
- a habit of constant goal-setting, about all aspects of the organisation's life, from individual performance goals to goals of meetings to goals of conversations
- the prevalence of strong relationships with a great deal of mutual recognition and respect
- there are only team bonuses, no individual ones
- a lot of reviews with clients, exploring not just the overall delivery of a piece of work but also individuals' performance.

At the root of it all is a shared set of beliefs and values, which mirror the beliefs and values we identified in Chapter 4 as the ones an individual needs to be an effective coach.

So here is yet another barrier to establishing a coaching culture: organisations are not generally full of people who have these beliefs and values. They will be full of, and need to be full of, people with a whole range of beliefs and values.

As an example, a senior manager I came across recently was quite open about his belief in 'winning at all costs' and his pleasure at seeing 'the other guy lose'. This hardly sits well with focusing on helping someone else to achieve their goals. But his energy and aggressiveness were key to an organisation he had to turn around. He certainly wasn't a coach, but he was effective in what the organisation needed him to do at that time.

Lane 4 recruits people as much for their values and beliefs as for their knowledge, experience and skills. Few organisations do this in such a rigorous way, and even those that do often recruit according to values and beliefs that are very different from those that underpin coaching.

This is not intended to be a counsel of despair, however. Increasingly, organisations are looking for people who believe in teamwork rather than individualism, who are motivated by opportunity to build rapport with a wide range of colleagues and clients, who are committed to their own and other people's development. These values are a solid foundation for a coaching culture.

But what we are saying here, as we have said throughout this book, is that effective coaching depends on the underlying beliefs and values of the coach. When we are wanting to introduce a coaching culture in which, essentially, everyone is a coach, we need to take a long, hard look at the underlying organisational beliefs and values.

Sometimes organisations go about this backwards, in my view. They want the governing beliefs and values to change (from competitiveness to collaboration, for example) and they think the introduction of coaching will produce that effect. But while there are still strong forces in the organisation encouraging competitiveness (recruitment process, promotion practices, reward systems) competitiveness will remain and coaching will not 'take'.

One of the things that stands out about Lane 4's approach to establishing its coaching culture is that it includes all aspects of company life. It is not merely window-dressing on a funda-

> ... effective coaching depends on the underlying beliefs and values of the coach.

mentally differently motivated organisation.

The challenge of giving people confidence they can coach

Because coaching has been taken up by so many 'professional coaches' (of whom I am one!), there can be a challenge in getting people to understand that everyone can and does coach – when their beliefs, values and motives are right. And for a coaching culture to be established (as opposed to a willingness of the part of the organisation to spend a lot of money on external coaches), what is needed is widespread confidence in and commitment to coaching.

I ran a training programme on coaching in an organisation recently where managers were genuinely concerned that they couldn't do such a good job as 'the professionals'. The coaching that goes on between colleagues is different from that between an employee and a professional external coach, that is true, but it is more valuable (and much more accessible) in many situations.

The way to meet this challenge, of giving people confidence, is by demystifying coaching. Training courses should encourage people to identify all the different sorts of coaching they have given and received in life. Coaching should be included as a standard activity on such things as appraisal forms.

In many ways, it is not a good idea to try to establish a coaching culture by introducing a large number of external providers – that can reinforce the impression that coaching is a specialist, rather than a common human, activity.

The challenge of having more than a coaching relationship with a coachee

One last, and important, challenge needs to be acknowledged. It is a challenge that Lane 4 is itself still wrestling with.

In Chapter 21, 'The player-coach', we talked about the challenge of having more than just a coaching relationship with a coachee. This challenge is even greater when an organisation is trying to establish a 'coaching culture'. Because that means there will be all sorts of relationships into which coaching needs to fit: boss–subordinate, partner–partner, 'front office–back-office', colleague–colleague, client–supplier, and so on.

Sometimes effective coaching will require an action that is difficult in the context of the current relationship. Lane 4, for example, is wrestling with the issue of people giving each other sufficiently honestly tough feedback. The strong relationships between people are an essential part of the fabric of the company. There is anxiety, and rightly so, about damaging those relationships.

You may remember Brendan Venter's advice on this challenge – depersonalise feedback by basing it on objective standards. It's good advice. But it's hard to do in the context of constant and informal coaching between people who work together. Also, it may lead us to miss out on some of the most valuable bits of feedback, feedback that takes the form 'I was just imagining how I might have been feeling if I had been the client in your presentation...'

A coaching culture is not the same thing as a cosy culture. In fact, it demands a high level of self-awareness and self-belief in the people who are part of it. It also demands the skills to have 'difficult conversations' with each other and through them develop rather than damage their relationships. Acknowledging this challenge is probably two-thirds of the way to helping people meet it.

> *A coaching culture is not the same thing as a cosy culture. In fact, it demands a high level of self-awareness and self-belief in the people who are part of it. It also demands the skills to have 'difficult conversations' with each other.*

As we have seen throughout this book, when people are clear about what they have to do, they are remarkably resourceful in working out how to do it. The real danger lies in presenting coaching as an easy add-on to existing professional relationships.

The opportunities, and how to capitalise on them

The opportunities of a coaching culture are so clear and so compelling that organisations continue, despite the serious challenges we have just identified, to aspire to such a culture.

When the Gallup organisation conducted a piece of research with over a million employees in a broad range of companies, industries and countries into the core characteristics an organisation needs to attract, focus, and keep the most talented employees (*First Break All the Rules* by Buckingham and Coffman, 1999), they discovered that what those talented employees wanted was to do what they do best, to be cared about as a person, to have their development encouraged, and to have opportunities to learn and grow. All these things are natural outcomes of effective coaching.

When Hay/McBer researched the leadership styles that have the biggest positive impact on climate (which is in its turn the biggest driver of organisational performance), they found that one of the two top styles was 'coaching' (defined as focusing on helping an employee improve their performance or develop long-term strengths) (see Goleman 2000).

These are just two examples of proven benefits of coaching; there are many others.

What this means is that even when an organisation does not succeed in establishing a company-wide coaching culture (and we have seen just how challenging that is), even small increases in the willingness and ability to coach of people at any level are likely to pay dividends.

Summary of tips for an organisation wanting to establish a 'coaching culture'

1 Build experience of and belief in coaching among the leaders of the organisation: the most effective move may be for the leadership team to receive coaching.

2 Capitalise on any experience of and belief in coaching at any influential levels of the organisation.

3 Get people talking about how coaching has helped them.

4 Clarify what a 'coaching culture' actually means: what would people be seeing, saying, doing and feeling that they're not now?

5 Take a long hard look at the organisation's existing culture. What needs to change for it to be compatible with coaching? Look especially at recruitment, promotion and reward.

6 Don't expect to 'sell' the idea solely on the basis of general research into the effects of coaching. The link between coaching and doing business is still far from obvious to many people.

7 Provide evidence that coaching has an impact on performance. Experiment with introducing a lot more coaching into a part of the organisation where its effects can be measured.

8 Demystify coaching; don't let people think it is the preserve of 'specialists'.

9 Acknowledge the difficulties of coaching people you work with. Encourage and help people to develop their skills at handling 'difficult conversations'.

10 Don't give up! Even small moves in the direction of a coaching culture can have big benefits.

References and Bibliography

BELBIN, R.M. (1993) *Team Roles at Work.* Oxford: Butterworth Heinemann

BION, W.R. (1961) *Experiences in Groups: and other papers.* London: Tavistock Publications

BOYATZIS, R. (1982) *The Competent Manager; a model for effective performance.* New York: John Wiley and Sons

BRIGGS MYERS, I. with MYERS, P.B. (1995) *Gifts Differing: understanding personality type.* Palo Alto: Davies-Black Publishing

BUCKINGHAM, M. and COFFMAN, C. (1999) *First, Break All the Rules: what the world's greatest managers do differently.* London: Simon & Schuster

BUZAN, T. and BUZAN, B. (1993) *The Mind Map Book.* London: BBC Books

CAMERON, J. (1992) *The Artist's Way: a spiritual path to higher creativity.* New York: Penguin Putnam

FLAHERTY, J. (1999) *Coaching – evoking excellence in others.* Oxford: Butterworth Heinemann

FROST, P.J. (2003) *Toxic Emotions at Work: how compassionate managers handle pain and conflict.* Boston: Harvard Business School Publishing

GALLWEY, W.T. and KRIEGEL, R. (1997) *Inner Skiing.* New York: Random House

GOFFEE, R. and JONES, G. (2000) 'Why should anyone be led by you?' *Harvard Business Review*, September–October

GOLEMAN, D. (1998) *Working with Emotional Intelligence.* London: Bloomsbury

GOLEMAN, D. (2000) 'Leadership that gets results', *Harvard Business Review,* March–April

HARDINGHAM, A. (1995) *Working in Teams.* London: Institute of Personnel and Development

HARDINGHAM, A. and ELLIS, C. (1999) *Exercises for Team Development.* London: Institute of Personnel and Development

HARDINGHAM, A. and ROYAL, J. (1994) *Pulling Together: teamwork in practice.* London: Institute of Personnel and Development

HARRIS, T.A. (1995) *I'm OK – You're OK.* London: Arrow Books

JACKSON, P. and ROSEN, C. (2002) *More Than a Game.* London: Simon & Schuster

KETS DE VRIES, M.F.R. and MILLER, D. (1984) *The Neurotic Organization: diagnosing and changing counterproductive styles of management.* San Francisco: Jossey-Bass

LANDSBERG, M. (1997) *The Tao of Coaching: boost your effectiveness at work by inspiring and developing those around you.* London: HarperCollins

MAISTER, D.H., GREEN, C.H. and GALFORD, R.M. (2002) *The Trusted Advisor.* London: Simon & Schuster

MINUCHIN, S. and FISHMAN, C.H. (1981) *Family Therapy Techniques.* Cambridge, Mass: Harvard University Press

O'CONNELL, B. (1998) *Solution-focused Therapy.* London: Sage

O'CONNOR, J. and McDERMOTT, I. (1996) *Thorson's Principles of NLP.* London: HarperCollins.

O'SULLIVAN R. (2004) *Ronnie: the autobiography of Ronnie O'Sullivan,* rev. edn. London: Orion Books

ROGERS, C.R. (1951) *Client-centered Therapy.* London: Constable

ROSEN, S. (1991) *My Voice Will Go With You: the teaching tales of Milton H. Erickson.* New York: Norton

SCHEIN, E.H. (1992) *Organizational Culture and Leadership.* San Francisco: Jossey-Bass

SCHUTZ, W. (1994) *The Human Element: productivity, self-esteem, and the bottom line.* San Francisco: Jossey-Bass

SCHWARZ, R. (2002) *The Skilled Facilitator: a comprehensive resource for consultants, facilitators, managers, trainers, and coaches.* San Francisco: Jossey-Bass

SENGE, P.M., KLEINER, A., ROBERTS, C., ROSS, R.B. and SMITH, B.J. (1994) *The Fifth Discipline Fieldbook: strategies and tools for building a learning organization.* London: Nicholas Brealey

STONE, D., PATTON, B. and HEEN, S. (2000) *Difficult Conversations: how to discuss what matters most.* London: Penguin Books

WINSTON, R. (2003) *The Human Mind: and how to make the most of it.* London: Bantam Press

Index